FADLEY

The Martz Connection

Peter and Alice Martz of Cresaptown,
Their Children,
And Their Children's Children

GARY FADLEY

RESEARCHER AND EDITOR: CYNTHIA BRAY

Copyright © 2016 Gary Fadley

All rights reserved.

ISBN:1542811740
ISBN-13: 9781542811743

Peter Martz
Margareth Adelhaid *Wigger* Martz

ABOUT THE COVER:

The cover is derived from this photo that pictures Peter and Alice (right) standing on the porch of that which I have come to believe is the old "Matz Place" in Cresaptown. The name of "Matz" was a corruption of "Martz" as English speakers attempted the German pronunciation of "Martz."

My uncertainty of the location pictured here, unfortunately, was not abated by Marshal Porter's caption of this picture in his book *Hallowed Be This Land,* a description that is verbatim thus:

> "*Right,* Mr. and Mrs. Peter Martz. *Left,* Daughter Margaret and young family on the porch of their old home."

Mr. Porter knew Peter and Alice and was their neighbor. Regrettably, however, his description of this photo is worded such that allows for uncertainty regarding the pronoun and its antecedent, though ambiguity and uncertainty are specters we always grapple with when investigating ancestors who deserve every diligence from those of us who endeavor to preserve their history.

In Latin, the Official Church Record Regarding the Burial of Peter Martz:

> Die 14 mensis Novemb. A. D. 1909 obiit Petrus Maertz
> filius Martini et Annae Maertz aetatis 80 ann.
> ex loco Cresaptown, sepultus est die 16 mens. Nov. A. D. 1909
> in cemeterio S. Ambrosii, Cresaptown, Md.
> Adnotationes Cancer
>   P. Thomas OFMCap.-

↓

TRANSLATION:

> On the 14th day of the month of November 1909 A.D. died Peter Martz
> the son of Martin and Anna Martz, age 80 years
> from Cresaptown, buried this 16th day of November 1909
> in the cemetery of St. Ambrose, Cresaptown, Md.
> The notes: Cancer
>   P. Thomas OFM Cap.

As Latin is a highly inflected language with a challenging number of conjugations and declensions, let the reader who doesn't understand Latin know hereby that the above "Petrus Maertz" is a Latin reference to "Peter Martz," and that "Martini et Annae" refers to "Martin and Anna."

The significance of this official church record, other than its preservation of the basic facts of his death, is that this is thus far the most reliable documentation I have found of the parents of Peter Martz, Martin and Anna, the mother and father he had left behind in Germany when he set out to make for himself a new life in a new world. I consider it reliable because it was almost certainly Alice herself who provided the priest with this information when she buried her husband.

THE MARTZ CONNECTION

Dedicated to the memory of

Peter Martz 1829 - 1909
July 22, 1829 - November 14, 1909

and his wife

Margareth *Wigger* Martz 1836 - 1913
Margareth Adelhaid *Wigger* Martz (called "Alice")

January 23, 1836 - January 27, 1913

BOTH BORN IN GERMANY

AND BOTH BURIED IN CRESAPTOWN, MARYLAND

1981 Re-issue of 1854 Certificate

Certificate of Marriage

Church of _SS. Peter & Paul, 125 Fayette St., Cumberland, Md. 21502_

This is to Certify That _Peter Martz_ and _Margaretha Adel. Wigger_ were lawfully Married on the _12_ day of _February_ 1854 According to the Rite of the Roman Catholic Church and in conformity with the laws of the State of _Maryland_

Rev. _VandeBraak_ officiating, in the presence of _Martin J. Zeller_ and _Elisabeth Schelhaus_ Witnesses, as appears from the Marriage Register of this Church.

Dated _7/15/81_

Rev. Rod Chesley, Pastor

Warning:
There are mistakes in the following obituary:

The Cumberland Alleganian, November 18, 1909

AGED CITIZEN DEAD

"Mr. Peter Martz died at his home at Winchester Bridge, aged 80 years. The deceased was a well known farmer of the district, wherein he spent the best years of his life. Death came to him at his home, which is situated between the bridge and Cresaptown.

Mr. Martz is survived by his wife, several children, grandchildren, and great-grandchildren. His immediate surviving relatives are the following daughters: Mrs. Margaret Michner, who was with her father when he died, Mrs. Julius Grabenstein, and Mrs. Barbara Bock, of Winchester Bridge; Mrs. John McBee of Cresaptown, and sons Mr. Bernard Martz, of this city, and Misters Peter, Martin, and Henry Martz, of Winchester Bridge. Mr. George Martz, sheriff of the county, is a cousin of the deceased. One daughter, Mrs. Kate Difenger, resides at Syracuse, New York."

Caveat:

The above obituary, copied verbatim from the newspaper, is incorrect on several accounts. Specifically: "Mrs. Margaret <u>Michner</u>" refers to Margaret <u>Metzner</u>. "Kate <u>Difenger</u>" is Kate <u>Duffner</u>. And "<u>Barbara Bock</u>" can only be <u>Anna Boch</u>, although Anna had a daughter named Barbara.

I can only imagine these mistakes to be the result of communication difficulties, written or verbal, between a newspaper employee and a grieving, stressed family with poor handwriting and a heavy German accent. The names, however, are correct in the following Table of Contents:

CONTENTS:

Peter Martz 1829 - 1909 x

Margareth Wigger Martz 1836 - 1913 x

Attack on The 21st Bridge 22

Mary Catherine Martz Grabenstein 1855 - 1924 36

    Anna M. Grabenstein 1885 - 1929 42

    Mary Clara Grabenstein Winter 1887 - 1970 45

    Peter Henry Grabenstein 1889 - 1961 49

    Elizabeth Mary Grabenstein McKenzie 1893 - 1961 58

    Herman Joseph Grabenstein 1893 - 1960 61

    Bernard Edward Grabenstein 1895 - 1966 65

    Nellie C. Grabenstein Barton 1898 - 1973 67

Johannes Martz 1858 - 1890 69

    Lucy Martz 1887 - 1894 74

    John W. Martz 1889 - 1920 75

Anna Catherine Martz Boch 1860 - 1919 77

    John Julius Boch 1884 - 1962 80

    George Henry Boch 1886 - 1943 82

    Catherine Elizabeth Boch McKenzie 1888 - 1970 88

    Agnes Ann Boch 1891 - 1900 91

    Anna Elizabeth Boch 1893 - 1901 91

    Bernard Joseph Boch 1896 - 1973 92

Mary Barbara Boch Condon 1896 - 1945 93

Frances Cecelia Boch Grabenstein 1898 - 1980 95

Joseph Edward Boch 1900 - 1901 96

Heinrich Wilhelm Martz 1863 - 1914 101

Edward Henry Martz 1892 - 1976 106

Harman Julius Martz 1894 - 1983 108

Marie Helen Martz Stewart 1896 - 1986 110

Francis Joseph Martz 1898 - 1984 112

Anna Josephine Martz 1902 - 1902 115

Elizabeth Catherine Martz Holt 1907 - 2007 119

Johannes Bernhart Martz 1865 - 1941 121

William Bernard Martz 1891 - 1941 125

Ralph Andrew Martz 1897 - 1926 127

Martin Joseph Martz 1869 - 1946 131

Joseph Francis Martz 1893 - 1910 136

Frederick Martin Martz 1895 - 1980 138

George Andrew Martz 1896 - 1966 142

Lucille Cecelia Martz 1897 - 1974 144

Charles Edward Martz 1899 - 1974 147

Clara Catherine Martz Poisal 1902 - 1961 149

Clarence Julius Martz 1903 - 1951 150

James Bernard Martz 1905 - 1953 151

Mary Margaret Martz Athey 1908 - 1979 152

Lawrence Aloysius Martz 1909 - 1923 153

Ursula Lillian Martz Kuhlman 1911 - 2001 154

John Martz 1913 - 1913 155

Peter Martin Martz 1870 - 1950 .... *157*

    Pearl Alice Martz Hill 1898 - 1987 .... *166*

    Julius William Martz 1900 - 1991 .... *175*

    Franklin Edward Martz 1903 - 1981 .... *185*

    Carolina Cecelia Martz Boyd 1906 - 1989 .... *204*

    Bertie Edna Martz Niner 1913 - 2012 .... *210*

    Peter Willard Martz 1916 - 2004 .... *212*

Catherine Elizabeth Martz Duffner 1874 - 1951 .... *217*

    Marie Magdelene Duffner Cady 1904 - 1991 .... *225*

Margaret Adelinde Martz Metzner 1877 - 1949 .... *230*

    Peter "Martz" Robinson 1895 - 1899 .... *235*

    Joseph Edward Metzner 1898 - 1978 .... *239*

    Marie Cecelia Metzner Holt 1901 - 1984 .... *241*

    Leo Henry Metzner 1906 - 1970 .... *243*

    Agnes Metzner Swisher 1909 - 1984 .... *244*

    Andrew Herman Metzner 1910 - 1990 .... *246*

    Margaret Ann Metzner Bucklew 1919 - 2003 .... *251*

Frances Cecilia Martz McBee 1880 - 1964 .... *253*

    Frances Cecilia McBee 1905 - 1906 .... *260*

    John Edward McBee 1907 - 1974 .... *263*

    Clarence Albert McBee 1909 - 1993 .... *266*

    Elizabeth Regina McBee Lupis 1912 - 2005 .... *268*

    Rosetta Mary McBee Amann 1915 - 2005 .... *269*

    Henry Bernard McBee 1918 - 1918 .... *271*

    Russell William McBee 1919 - 1989 .... *272*

    Margaret Catherine McBee Sudine 1923 - 1994 .... *275*

In Memoriam

It is always right and proper that we remember and thank all those brave and noble souls who went before us, establishing our rich traditions, forming the foundations on which we continue to build, encouraging us by the way they survived their hardships and celebrated their lives, bequeathing to us Life itself in these glorious-if-challenging mountains.

In particular, however, it is my solemn wish that this book will serve to perpetuate the memory of the children who left us much too soon:

Eddie Martz, Earl Martz, Helen Martz, Peter Martz, Paul Martz, Ralph Martz, Joseph Martz, Anna Josephine Martz, Lawrence Martz, Lucy Martz, John Martz, Peter "Martz" Robinson, Dorothy Winter, Infant Grabenstein, Martha Veronica Grabenstein, Agnes Ann Boch, Anna Elizabeth Boch, Joseph Edward Boch, Frances McBee, Henry McBee, Infant Kuhlman twins, Stillborn Kuhlman Infant, and all the babies who died before being named, and all the other children of the Martz Connection who did not survive their childhoods, each of inestimable value, each an integral part of this amazing totality called Humanity. This is who we are.

The Martz Connection

Introduction

In 2014, my story "Attack on The 21st Bridge" was published in *Journal of The Alleghenies*. It's my version of a story that describes a U.S. Civil War battle just south of Rawlings, Maryland, a battle involving my ancestors, the Peter and Alice Martz family.

Early in 2015, subsequent to the story's appearance in the journal, the president of the *Genealogical Society of Allegany County*, Doctor Anthony Crosby, invited me to speak at the March meeting of the Society, asking me to present to the Society my knowledge of the Martz family. I was, of course, quite honored by the invitation and agreed to be the guest speaker at the March meeting.

Next, immediately upon agreeing to speak to the Society, I launched a considerable research into the Martz side of my family. Then, on March 19, 2015, I rendered my presentation to the Society, and this at hand is the result and evolution of my preparation for that presentation.

Specifically, this is information I acquired or corroborated via historic newspapers, family archives, *the Social Security Death Index*, the *U.S. Census*, personal interviews, and many visits to libraries, parish offices, and cemeteries. However, other than information of which I have personal knowledge, and other than concrete evidence such as headstones, I can only report the imperfect record. After all, even a relatively-official newspaper obituary can provide only that information proffered by imperfect humanity, and, even then, a typing error can perpetuate misinformation. Yet it remains my hope and intention that this book will be helpful to anyone seeking the stories of those within its pages.

The woeful lack of available information was a bit discouraging at first, so I soon became very grateful for every piece of knowledge that some of our diligent and thoughtful ancestors have bequeathed to us by way of photographs, obituaries, documents, and oral tradition.

In most cases, I am reasonably certain that the given lists of descendants are complete. In other cases, however, I can report only on that information that I was able to discover. We know that Peter Martz had ten children; his historical prominence has generated credible records of his life and progeny. Also, certain newspaper obituaries have preserved the facts regarding some of his "children's children," but in some cases I was unable to find any newspaper article or other credible artifact to corroborate information gleaned from less-official sources. The point of all of this, of course, is to alert the reader to the fact that any given list of children's children, unless the certainty of that list is stated, might be incomplete. That's a point I wish to stress with all gravity, for certainly we would deeply regret losing *anyone* through the sieve of history.

Another thing is this: The spelling of proper names was never a science. People spell their names however they will, and certainly they cannot control how others might spell them. Additionally, immigrants sometimes take on other names or spellings that might be more compatible with the culture in which they find their existence. All of this is why I have decided on my own rule: I have decided, that is, that the name on one's gravestone is the name the deceased had settled with, for I just feel it unlikely that a family would actually pay a lapidary to commit a "grave mistake," if you will excuse the pun. And not only the *names* but also the *dates of birth and death* that are inscribed in gravestones are the dates I have committed to record, absolutely astonished at the abundance of misinformation I have discovered on certain websites, misinformation that in some cases I was able to disregard to my own satisfaction only by going to graves and reading the stones.

In our research, my wife and I had the good fortune of locating and meeting Helen *Amann* Hannon, Kitty *McBee* Mitchell, and Teresa *Lupis* Savage, all of them granddaughters of Frances *Martz* McBee, called "Fannie." Fannie was the 10th and last child born to Peter and Alice. These very cordial, very provident granddaughters of Fannie Martz were a great help toward the production of this book.

Fannie's daughter, Elizabeth *McBee* Lupis, apparently had a keen sense of family and cared as much to obtain a re-issue of Peter's and Alice's marriage certificate, as well as the baptism certificates for all ten of their children. Furthermore, Elizabeth wrote copious notes recording family marriages, births, baptisms, and deaths. I am eternally grateful to Elizabeth for securing these priceless facts and documents, and I am equally grateful to Teresa for providing me with copies of it all. Those re-issued certificates appear near the beginning of each child's section of this book.

For anyone not familiar with a "re-issue" of a church document, let me explain. For example, if you should lose your original baptism certificate, you need only request another from your pastor, who can then acquire the original information from the ledger in which a former pastor had recorded the sacrament. One problem is that the original information was sometimes entered hastily by the hand of a busy priest who might have virtually *scribbled* the information, which, due to faulty deciphering, might many years later be the source of misinformation. So, to borrow from the Latin that every priest knew, *caveat emptor*, "let the buyer beware." Also, the census takers who were equally busy and just as prone to scribbling, have left us with a record that has often been carelessly deciphered and sometimes misinterpreted, so we must always keep these things in mind and not become vexed or misled in our effort to understand the details of the past. Instead, however, even though this text is supported by considerable documentation, let's put aside the rigors of empirical investigation and proceed with the fascinating discovery of a dynamic and very interesting family whose blood continues to pulse through these marvelous mountains.

THE MARTZ CONNECTION

Attack on The 21st Bridge

A Short Story
About The Beginning of The Peter Martz Family in Allegany County, Maryland

That which follows is a story I constructed from the reminiscing and storytelling of my ancestors, the diligent records of great historians such as J. Marshall Porter, the generous contributions from the clear memories of Catherine E. *Boch* McKenzie, as bequeathed by her provident grandson, Joseph McKenzie, and official Civil War Records. Catherine E. *Boch* McKenzie is the daughter of Anna *Martz* Boch, and Anna was the youngest survivor of the Confederate attack on the 21st Bridge in Allegany County during the U.S. Civil War.

If you should find any enjoyment in reading this very true story, then I am pleased as a writer. It was not, however, merely for entertainment that I wrote this story. Instead, I wrote it simply because I would not be here if Peter Martz and Alice Wigger had not each taken the bold step of immigrating here from Germany, and for that—for giving me life in these sweet mountains—I will return whatever I can, which isn't much, but at least I can tell and preserve that which I know of their story. By *that* I mean the story of their lives together, a perpetual union of which we have records that date back at least to their marriage in 1854 and to the horror that befell their home in 1861 during the devastating attack on the 21st Bridge.

The 21ˢᵗ Bridge was a railroad bridge over the Potomac between Cumberland and Keyser near High Rock, 21 miles west of Cumberland, hence the 21ˢᵗ Bridge.

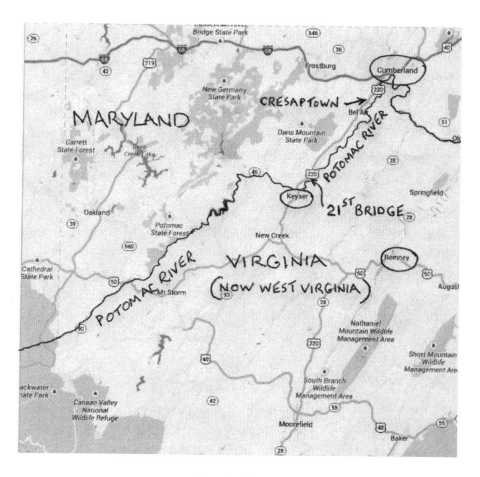

Reminder:

There was no West Virginia before the Civil War, so that state across the river from Allegany County was Virginia.

Attack on The Twenty-First Bridge

Like a lot of people in those days, Peter Martz had virtually fled to America from Germany, from poverty, oppression, and the repercussions of a failed revolution, hoping to find in the "New World" a new way of life complete with all the security and implied promises of a great democracy. It was 1850, and, at the age of twenty-one, Peter Martz had settled in mountainous Western Maryland, trusting in Divine Providence, a strong German will, and the nurturing soil of the Potomac River Valley south of Cumberland.

Divine Providence, however, had not yet established a Catholic Church there in that fertile valley the lay nestled between the mammoth Dan's Mountain in Maryland and the rolling Knobley Mountain in West Virginia. We can imagine, therefore, even though his Protestant friends were surely blessing him with their normal charity and predictable hospitality, that the Catholic Peter Martz set out on his new life with a certain loneliness that might be fully understood only by a staunch Catholic who must go about without the comforting presence of the priest-consecrated Holy Eucharist and without the reassurance and fortification of routinely accessible Sunday Masses.

There were, however, sweet and splendid Catholic Churches in nearby Cumberland, though nothing was actually "nearby" in those days in which people got about on horses or in horse-drawn wagons that were not always up to the challenge of dirt roads that were dominated by mud, rocks, ruts, and snowdrifts.

By the 1850's Cumberland had become a major center of commerce and transportation. Such a city's growing population, many of whom were Catholic immigrants, prompted the building of those heretofore mentioned "sweet and splendid" Catholic Churches, one of which was SS Peter & Paul on Fayette Street in Cumberland, the church founded by Saint John Neumann, America's first male saint. And this was the church where in 1854 Peter Martz married Margareth Adelhaid Wigger, herself a German immigrant who here in the New World would go by the name of "Alice," and in the next year, 1855, Alice gave birth to Peter Martz's first child, a healthy baby girl whom they called Mary Catherine.

Peter soon began working for the Baltimore and Ohio Railroad Company, and when the Civil War began in 1861, he was working as a B&O watchman at the Twenty-First Bridge, where the railroad crossed the Potomac River between Cumberland and Keyser, which in those days was known as "New Creek." They lived in a house adjacent to the bridge, facilitating Peter's day and night vigilance as keeper of the bridge, and by 1861 the Martz family had grown with the addition of two more children: Johannes, born in 1858, and Anna Catherine, born 1860.

The challenges of attending to a six-year-old, a three-year-old, and a baby amount to sufficient stress, but now the country to which Peter and Alice had fled for their peace and security was in the turmoil of its own devastating civil war.

The railroads, of course, were the arteries by which the men, cannons, ammunition, and supplies were routed for the purpose of either aggression or defense, depending on which side one was on, which is why the standard protocol of war called for the destruction of the railroad bridges and the destruction of the rails, with the destruction of the bridges being obviously the greater goal, as it took forever to rebuild a bridge, especially when the builders were under enemy fire.

As Peter Martz left virtually nothing in writing, and as we have no one who knew him personally, and as it seems he has bequeathed absolutely no political opinions, we just cannot say that the man was either a Rebel or a Yankee. We just don't know what his sentiments and loyalties might have been. Being a recent immigrant, it is likely that he had little time to be either brainwashed or enlightened, again depending on which side he was on, if any. It is, in fact, more likely that Peter Martz was simply a man with a family to protect and with a bridge to guard.

Early in 1861, after the Confederates had destroyed bridges over the North Branch of the Potomac, other bridges over nearby Patterson's Creek, and still others farther east and west, a military company was recruited from among the able-bodied men in and around Cumberland, and, being commissioned with the impressive name of the "Cumberland Continentals," their mission was to guard and defend the railroad and canal structures between Hancock and Keyser.

A contingent of these Cumberland Continentals were stationed at the Twenty-First Bridge, where they were living in railroad camp-cars and eating the meals that Alice Martz was preparing for them every day. And now, in addition to his guard duties for the B&O, a guard duty in which he was now being aided by Union soldiers, Peter Martz was butchering his own animals and curing meat for the soldiers' mess, as well as feeding them vegetables and grain from his own gardens and fields. From the deep pockets of Mr. Lincoln's Union, Peter Martz would perhaps be compensated for his provisions and services, though we have no reason to doubt that the brave men in *grey* would have received the same hospitality, for we should never doubt that a good and grateful Christian man would have done the very same even without recompense and without regard to which side of this miserable conflict his peculiar guests were obliged to serve.

On the evening of June 18, 1861, when Peter and Alice Martz tucked in their three children and then themselves retired from another busy and anxious day, they could not have known that Confederate Colonel A.P. Hill, commanding the 13th Virginia Infantry, had earlier in the day directed Colonel J.C. Vaughn of the 3rd Tennessee (then at Romney) to take two companies from his own and two from the 13th Virginia Regiment and to proceed to Keyser and to kill or disperse the Union guards and to burn the Twenty-First Bridge.

THE MARTZ CONNECTION

On the morning of June 19, 1861, Peter Martz was out of bed and moving about his farm with the first streaks of dawn, as he always had done, because that's what farmers and watchmen do. The days had become monotonous for Peter since the outbreak of the war two months earlier, attending to farming and to troops, going through each day wondering and worrying about the safety of his wife and children, almost trying to convince himself that the Twenty-First Bridge would never be attacked. And, apparently, the troops stationed there at the bridge had themselves become weary to the point of letting their guard down, for Peter had noticed they had posted no pickets, and some of them had actually obtained passes to go home, so there were a mere twenty-eight tired and assuming Union troops at the bridge that fateful morning in June so many years ago.

In the shallow light of summer morning, carrying a burlap sack of cracked corn, Peter was headed for the chicken coop when he noticed a commotion about the bridge and camp cars. Several of the Continentals had spotted strangers coming over the brow of Bullneck Hill on the Virginia side of the Potomac. Then firing began almost immediately, and the great number of shots that rang out from the river and fields told Peter Martz that the soldiers at the bridge were woefully outnumbered. But it wasn't until one of the Continentals fell wounded near the house that Peter called for Alice and told her it was time to clear out.

The fighting was fierce when Alice took the two older children, six-year-old Mary Catherine and three-year-old Johannes, and ran to the home of a neighbor, the Ravencraft home, through a deep cut and out of the line of fire. Peter took the baby, little Anna, and began crawling through a grain field, while bullets whistled and whizzed over their heads until father and baby were out of sight of the house.

The raging battle continued for some time that morning until the Confederates had routed the Union troops and had taken control of the bridge and the Martz property. The Martzes took refuge perhaps in the Ravencraft home, though it is more likely that they all stayed in hiding somewhere on or near the Ravencraft property, hoping and praying that the Ravencraft home would not be the next target. If so, their prayers were answered, for the Confederate troops had not pursued the Martzes, and the Ravencraft home was untouched.

The Martz family did not venture back to their house until that night, but when they got there they saw the devastating effects of the day's horrible events. They found their house in shambles. All their meat and canned goods and other provisions were gone. The bridge and the camp cars and crossties were still burning. A half mile of tracks on the Maryland side was torn up, and the rails were twisted around trees and fence posts. There was not a Union soldier in sight. And it was right then and there, while gazing upon the burning wreckage that only hours ago had been his life and livelihood, that Peter Martz decided to move.

The very next day, June 20, 1861, amidst acrid smoke, smoldering timbers, and a surreal landscape, Peter Martz packed up his wife and children and headed north toward Cumberland, settling on a thirty acre parcel of poor, hilly land near Cresaptown. This re-start for the Martz family was two miles into the woods between Winchester Road and Dan's Mountain, and this was the homestead that for many generations to come would be known as the "Matz Place." Presumably, the name of "Matz" was an English corruption as Cresaptown locals attempted to assimilate the spelling and sound of the German name "Martz," and this writer is one of the many in Cresaptown who grew up hearing of "the old Matz Place."

Peter continued working for the B&O Railroad, employed in Cresaptown at the flag-stop known as Brady Station, and, although we don't know the details of just how he came to acquire "the old Matz Place," we know that he soon planted hundreds of cherry trees on those hills and in those rocky fields, and we know that his trees were soon very successful. In his book *Hallowed Be This Land*, J. Marshall Porter, writing of "the old Matz Place," refers to "...hundreds of tall cherry trees that bore small red heart, pink heart and black heart cherries."

At "the old Matz Place," in a four-room house of logs that was heated by burning wood and lighted by burning oil, Alice gave birth to seven more children, so now there were <u>ten</u>:

Mary Catherine b.1855…Johannes b.1858…Anna Catherine b.1860…

Heinrich Wilhelm b.1863…Johannes Bernhart b.1865…

Martin Joseph b.1868…Peter Martin b.1870…

Catherine Elizabeth b.1874…Margaret Adelinde b.1877…

Frances Cecilia b.1880

We know this list of her children is complete, because Alice herself, at the age of 65 in the 1900 *U.S. Census,* declared she had given birth to a total of <u>ten</u> children in her lifetime.

J. Marshall Porter and others have expressed their curiosity as to how Peter and Alice managed to raise that many children in a four-room house. Who knows how much love, sacrifice, and devotion it takes to accomplish such a thing? One answer is that the children themselves have to be a part of the solution. And so they were. They all picked and sold cherries, but not only cherries, for the woods of Dan's Mountain and Haystack Mountain were abundant with blackberries and huckleberries that the Martz children must have brought in by the gallons in the fruitful days of Appalachian summer, and, in a horse-drawn spring wagon, Alice would take the harvest to market in nearby towns. Also, as the older children became able to go on any of the so-called "public works," they did so, and they donated their meager wages to the care of the younger children. But what a fine and encouraging sight they must have been each Sunday morning in a happy-if-crowded horse-drawn wagon, all dressed in their Sunday best, braving the rocky, rutted roads that led them to the Mass at SS Peter & Paul in Cumberland. And how happy they must have been when the Saint Ambrose Church was built in Cresaptown in 1886.

The children all grew up and moved on to lives of their own, however, which must have made the little house feel very large and empty for Peter and Alice. But such is life. By way of marriage, the Martz girls brought into the family other great names: Grabenstein, Boch, Duffner, Metzner, and McBee. And nearly all the Martz boys grew up to be railroad track-workers. One of them, Peter Martin Martz, became this writer's great-grandfather.

When Peter Martz died at the age of eighty in the fall of 1909, Alice continued to live at "the old Matz Place." She enjoyed the regular visits of her children, who by all accounts were very attentive to her needs, and one of the younger daughters moved her own family back into her mother's house, which must have been sweet company for Alice for a few years. In time, however, the long trek from the old Matz place to his work on the railroad became too much of a burden for that daughter's husband, so they had to move back to the home they had left. After that, Alice went to spend her last days in the home of a daughter, where she died in 1913.

Peter and Alice Martz are buried side-by-side on the gentle slope of Saint Ambrose Cemetery in Cresaptown, surrounded by many of the children and grandchildren who owe their proud German heritage to these two stalwarts of Appalachian character, real-life heroes who survived the rigors of hard life, who honored the everyday heroism to which every mother and father are called, and, drawn into circumstances beyond their control, survived even the devastating Civil War and the life-changing attack on their home at the 21st Bridge.

**21st Bridge Road
Intersects With RT. 220
Between Rawlings and McCoole
Near High Rock**

The Cumberland Alleganian
February 18, 1904

Martz Anniversary

"On Friday Mr. and Mrs. Peter Martz celebrated the golden anniversary of their marriage at their home near Cresaptown.

The event was solemnized with a High Mass at Saint Ambrose Church, Cresaptown, at 10 a.m.. After this service, dinner was served at the home of this aging couple. Upwards of 150 relatives and neighbors joined in the feast.

Mr. Muir of Lonaconing interested the guests with many striking performances. Mr. Martz is upwards of 80 years of age, and his good wife, who has shared his happiness for fifty years, is past 75 years. Both still enjoy good health."

Margareth Adelhaid Wigger Martz
With Eight of Her Ten Children

Standing Left to Right:

Margaret Adelinde Metzner, Heinrich Wilhelm Martz,
Anna Catherine Boch, Peter Martin Martz,
Catherine Elizabeth Duffner, Johannes Bernhart Martz,
Mary Catherine Grabenstein, Frances Cecilia McBee

Or, as they were called,

Maggie, Henry,
Annie, Peter,
Kate, Bernard,
Mary Catherine, and Fannie

Not present in this early 1900's photo
are Johannes, who died in 1890,
and Martin Joseph, who is absent for unknown reasons.

The End of The Old "Matz" Place

After Peter Martz died in 1909, and after Alice died in 1913, the old Matz Place was put up for sale. It fell to the oldest daughter, Mary Catherine *Martz* Grabenstein to conduct the business of selling her deceased parents' property, but, of course, business was usually conducted by *men* in those days, so it was Mary Catherine's husband Julius who would manage the farewell to the old Martz family home:

Cumberland Evening Times, November 12, 1913

PUBLIC SALE
-OF-
VALUABLE FARM NEAR CRESAPTOWN

The undersigned will, on Saturday, November 15, 1913, at 11 o'clock a.m., on the City Hall Square at the corner of Little Frederick and North Center Streets, offer at public sale to the highest bidder, all that farm and improvements located near Cresaptown, Md, known as the Peter Martz Farm, said farm being situated about 8 miles from Cumberland and about two miles from Cresaptown, and contains about 140 acres of land, more or less.

This farm is improved by a six-room frame dwelling with galvanized roof and good cellar, and other necessary outbuildings, all in good condition.

There are a number of fruit trees and about 10,000 mine props on the property.

TERMS OF SALE—Cash on day of sale.
For particulars, address:
Julius Grabenstein
Cumberland, Md., R.F.D. No. 1
Charles C. Wilson, Auctioneer

THE MARTZ CONNECTION

I

MARY CATHERINE

Mary Catherine *Martz* Grabenstein
1855 - 1924

(Daughter of Peter and Alice Martz)

September 12, 1855 - September 4, 1924

Buried at SS Peter and Paul Cemetery in Cumberland, she is the wife of Julius Grabenstein 1858 - 1930, with whom she had these seven children:

Anna 1885 - 1929

Mary 1887 - 1970

Peter 1889 - 1961

Elizabeth 1891 - 1961

Herman 1893 - 1960

Bernard 1896 - 1966

Nellie 1898 - 1973

1981 Re-issue of 1855 Certificate

Certificate of Baptism

Ss. Peter & Paul Church
125 FAYETTE STREET
CUMBERLAND, MARYLAND 21502

This is to Certify

That Maria Catharina (Maerz) Martz

Child of Peter Maerz

and Margaretha Adelheid Wigger

born in Cresaptown
(CITY)   (STATE)

on the 12 day of September 19 1855

was **Baptized**

on the 30 day of September 19 1855

According to the Rite of the Roman Catholic Church
by the Rev. VandeBraak

the Sponsors being: Bernard Wigger
                    Maria Cath. Welps

as appears from the Baptismal Register of this Church.

Dated 7/15/81

Rev. _____ Pastor

A Cumberland newspaper obituary declares Mary Catherine's husband to be "Louis" Grabenstein, which is incorrect according to all other sources, so I corrected the name in the obituary you will read, for surely his name is "Julius," a fact known to this writer, who is the great-grandson of Mary Catherine's brother. In other words, I knew people who knew him. Furthermore, the fact of his name is corroborated by other sources including historian J. Marshall Porter, the *U.S. Social Security Death Index* and the *U.S. Census,* and his name is made most certain by visiting his grave, where the rather impressive stone is still rather clearly marked as <u>Julius</u> .

Also on Mary Catherine's "memorial" that you might see on a popular website is a photo of Mary Catherine pictured standing with her mother Alice, and the photo is dated "1915," even though we know her mother died in 1913.

The point is that we must remain aware of the possibility or error with any source offering information. I've noticed, just for example, that some of the recorders of the *U.S. Census* had very poor handwriting and have left us with a sometimes-illegible record. Then the illegible or barely-legible record is interpreted by others who then record their interpretations as fact.

THE MARTZ CONNECTION

Mary Catherine:

Born September 12, 1855, Mary Catherine was the six-year-old survivor of the "Attack on The 21st Bridge" during the U.S. Civil War. She grew up to marry the son of another German immigrant, Julius Grabenstein, and, even while Julius worked as a railroad trackman and later as a foreman, she and Julius operated a farm on the Dan's Mountain side of Winchester Road, in the "Winchester Bridge" area, which was between Cresaptown and LaVale, where she and the children did much of the farming while Julius worked the railroad, as described by J. Marshall Porter in *Hallowed Be This Land*:

> "Mrs. Grabenstein, who was the daughter of Peter Martz, had known and done field work all her girl-hood life and was well fitted to clearing the hilly land her husband had taken her to when they were first married. There they built a house near a spring, and the barn not far below, and, while Mr. Grabenstein spent his days working on the railroad, Mrs. Grabenstein cleared the woods land they settled on. As the boys and girls grew up, they were taken to the fields to help their mother plow and plant and cultivate and harvest. A boy or girl rode the horse while the mother plowed, and others hoed or chopped sprouts in the new garden. And when the fruit or vegetables were ready for market, one of the boys or girls...."

Anyone interested in the incredible Mary Catherine *Martz* Grabenstein should read *Hallowed be This Land,* and should especially read its chapter 11, "The Julius Grabenstein Farm."

Mary Catherine died at home on Thursday, September 4, 1924, leaving Julius a widower until his death six years later on September 23, 1930 after raising the seven children listed in her obituary:

Cumberland Evening Times, Thursday, September 11, 1924:
(Corrected Version)

"The funeral of Mrs. Mary Grabenstein, aged 68 years, who died at her home last Thursday, was held from SS Peter & Paul Catholic Church, Cumberland, with Requiem Mass. Pallbearers were nephews: Edward Martz, Leo Metzner, George Fox, Julius Martz, William Martz, and George Martz.

Mrs. Grabenstein is survived by her husband, Julius Grabenstein and seven children: Misses Anna, Elizabeth, and Nellie of the home; Mrs. Mary Winter of Cresaptown, Peter H. Grabenstein, this place, and Herman and Bernard Grabenstein, Cumberland. The following brothers and sisters survive: Martin Martz, this place; Peter Martz, Cresaptown; Bernard Martz, Cumberland; Mrs. Kate Duffner, Syracuse, NY; Mrs. Frances McBee, Westernport, and Mrs. Margaret Metzner, Winchester Bridge."

The Winchester Road Farm of Julius and Mary Catherine *Martz* Grabenstein, where Mary Catherine and her children did much of the farming while Julius spent his days working the busy railroad.

The Death of Julius Grabenstein

After the death of Mary Catherine, Julius lived on another six years. In fact, after his wife's death in September of 1924, Julius would see exactly six more Septembers.

It's easy to imagine Julius' grief each September, as the month certainly would have reminded him of the grief of losing his life's partner, and, on the sixth September of his loneliness, Julius himself would surrender after having fought the good fight.

The Cumberland Alleganian
September 13, 1930

"Julius Grabenstein, Winchester Road, is seriously ill with pneumonia at Allegany Hospital where he has been a patient since Tuesday."

The Cumberland Alleganian
September 24, 1930

"Julius Grabenstein, 72, of Winchester Road, died yesterday afternoon at the Allegany Hospital, where he had been a patient more than two weeks. He is survived by six children: P. H. Grabenstein, Winchester Road; Harmon and Bernard Grabenstein, this city; Mrs. Wressell Winters of Cresaptown; Mrs. Harmon Barton of Pinto, and Mrs. William McKenzie at home."

The Children of Mary Catherine *Martz* Grabenstein:

Anna M. Grabenstein 1885 - 1929

(Daughter of Mary Catherine *Martz* Grabenstein)

September 23, 1885 - February 28, 1929

From the *Cumberland Evening Times* Obituary
Tuesday, March 5, 1929:

1. She was born on September 23, 1885.
2. She was a member of Saint Ambrose Parish in Cresaptown.
3. She was 43 years old.
4. She was devoted to caring for her aged father and to Church activities.
5. She was a worker in the *League of the Little Flower of Saint Theresa.*
6. She was a member of the *Sodality of The Blessed Virgin Mary.*
7. She was "Miss" Grabenstein, and there is no mention of a husband or children, leading me to presume that she had never been married, and that perhaps she lived a life of chastity, a promise to God that would have helped her focus on her religious life and dedicate her efforts to bringing Christ to the world.
8. She was well known and held in high esteem.
9. She died in Allegany Hospital on February 28, 1929.
10. Hundreds visited the Grabenstein home, where she lay in repose until her funeral, and the flower tributes were profuse and beautiful.
11. Her Requiem Mass was celebrated at SS Peter and Paul.
12. She is buried at SS Peter & Paul Cemetery.

After Anna died, the father she had cared for died on Anna's birthday the following year, September 23, 1930.

Anna is buried in the same plot with her mother, father, and sister Elizabeth. Anna's little stone repeatedly becomes buried and unseen, with grass growing over it, so remember that if you look for it.

The above is her stone that I photographed after uncovering it once my wife's probing found it beneath inches of earth. With little effort, one can read on it the inscribed name of "ANNA M."

This appeared to be a simple, flat stone into which is carved simply the name of "ANNA M," all upper-case letters. Such a stone, a thing of elegant simplicity, is to this writer at once a thing of great curiosity and perhaps a testimony of deep, devoted love.

Presenting her obituary information (above), I speculated regarding the possibility of her living a life of simplicity and perhaps even chastity, opting to be married to Christ and the Church instead of marriage and family. Such an honorable devotion was once very popular among some Christian women. My speculation is based also on her membership in the *Sodality of The Blessed Virgin Mary* and to her role as a worker in the *League of The Little Flower of Saint Theresa*.

I admit to this speculation in this book that otherwise endeavors to present only the facts, but your writer is a confessed romantic who finds it practically impossible to stay always within the empirical boundaries he earnestly tries to observe, so I allow myself this bit of sentimental musing when I imagine this unembellished stone to be a memorial to the beautifully modest soul of a woman who seems to have devoted her life to noble simplicity.

It was completely underground, but, upon uncovering it, I photographed a stone I thought to be the size of a common brick. However, some weeks later, my wife and I decided we should raise it up a little so its flat surface would be a couple inches above ground. This is normally accomplished by digging up the stone, packing some earth under it, and then replanting the stone, a task we ended up performing on many stones in the process of preparing pictures for this book.

We were surprised, however, at the depth of this stone, so, after more digging than we had expected, we replanted a stone that then stood nearly a full foot above ground and displayed the previously hidden lifespan of 1885 - 1929:

Mary Clara *Grabenstein* Winter 1887 - 1970
(Daughter of Mary Catherine *Martz* Grabenstein)

Mary Clara and her husband, Wressell Winter,
had the following twelve children:

William Edgar
Frances Edna
Joseph
Elmer
Kathleen
Ruth
Arthur "Bill"
Thomas
Louis
Harold
Delores
Dorothy

The above list of Mary Clara's children is complete and in order according to Ginger Winter, who is Mary Clara's granddaughter. Furthermore, this list is corroborated by the total *U.S. Census* record from 1910 to 1940, the years in which these children were born.

The importance of this list is in the fact that any obituary often does not list all of the decedent's children, instead listing only those who are surviving. Indeed, when we read the actual newspaper obituary for Mary Clara, as well as the one for Wressell, we read of only the surviving four daughters and six sons, though there were in fact five daughters and seven sons. The son not listed as surviving was Thomas, who in 1943, at the age of 19, was killed in an accident at work at the Glen Martin aircraft plant in Baltimore. And the daughter not listed in newspaper obituaries as surviving is Dorothy, Mary Clara's last-born child, who lived only several hours after being born.

Mary Clara *Grabenstein* Winter 1887 - 1970

From the *Cumberland Evening Times* Obituary of Tuesday, June 9, 1970, and from my interview of Ginger Winter, the granddaughter of Mary Clara *Grabenstein* Winter:

1. Mary Clara was born in the Winchester Bridge area.
2. She was born April 19, 1887.
3. She became the wife of <u>Wressell Osman Winter</u>.
4. She was a member of the United Methodist Church in Cresaptown, the Golden Rule Sunday School Class, and the Cresaptown Homemakers Club.
5. She died on June 8, 1970 after several years of ill health.
6. She was 83 years old when she died.
7. She was survived by four daughters:
   Ruth Niner, Edna Judy, Kate Chaney, Delores Shipe
8. She was preceded in death by a fifth daughter, Dorothy Winter.
9. She was survived by six sons:
   William, Joseph, Elmer, Arthur (Bill), Louis, Harold
10. She was preceded in death by a seventh son, Thomas.
11. Funeral Service was led by Rev. Harold McClay Jr.
12. She is buried at Hillcrest Memorial Park.

Mary Clara's husband bore the rather unusual name of "Wressell," a fact I mention here because his name has been in other places cited as "Wrussell" and as "Russell."

I grew up in a Cresaptown where I heard people pronounce his name as "Russell," but, in the process of my researching the facts for this book, I obtained from Wressell's granddaughter Ginger, the daughter of Arthur "Bill" Winters, that the correct spelling of her grandfather's name is "Wressell," and that is how it is spelled on his grave marker at Hillcrest Cemetery in Cumberland.

Your author is pleased to count among his friends and cousins many of Mary Clara's descendants, especially the Winter girls (Ginger, Cheryl, Ricky, and Kista), daughters of Arthur and granddaughters of Mary Clara *Grabenstein* Winter. Ginger Winter in particular was very helpful in this portion of this book.

Mary Clara's husband was <u>Wressell Osman Winter 1885 - 1964</u>, son of the industrious Elijah Winter 1850 - 1934. Elijah owned and operated a busy water-powered grist mill in Cresaptown in the 19th and 20th centuries and was one of the early pillars of the community. The water that turned the mill's huge wheel was Warrior Run, which for enumerable generations has coursed its way along Winchester Road and down through Cresaptown. Much of that water was runoff from the Martz and Grabenstein properties upstream, and those Martzes and Grabensteins would themselves routinely travel downstream to Elijah's mill, where he would turn their corn, wheat, rye, and buckwheat into useable meal or flour.

Here then is the obituary of Wressell Osman Winter, son of Elijah and husband of Mary Clara *Grabenstein* Winter:

Cumberland Evening Times, February 20, 1964

Wressell O. Winter

"Wressell Osman Winter, 78, of Cresaptown, died yesterday at Sacred Heart Hospital where he was admitted January 26. He had been in failing health seven years.

He was a son of the late Elijah and Eliza *Starkey* Winter.

He was an employee of Celanese Fiber Company in extrusion engineering before retiring in May 1954, and a member of Cresaptown Methodist Church.

Surviving are his wife, Mary Clara *Grabenstein* Winter; six sons, William E., Joseph M., Elmer R., Louis R., and Arthur E. Winter, all of Cresaptown, and Rev. Harold G. Winter, Wadsworth, Ohio; four daughters, Mrs. Edna Judy, Mrs. Kathleen Chaney, Mrs. Delores Shipe, Cresaptown, and Mrs. Ruth Niner, Pinto; 43 grandchildren and 26 great-grandchildren.

The body is at the John J. Hafer Chapel of the Hills Mortuary, where friends will be received today from 7 to 9 p.m. and tomorrow from 2 to 4 and 7 to 9 p.m.

A service will be conducted there Saturday at 2 p.m. by Rev. William Balderson. Interment will be in Hillcrest Memorial Park."

Peter Henry Grabenstein 1889 - 1961

(Son of Mary Catherine *Martz* Grabenstein)

Married to <u>Delores *Metzner* Grabenstein 1889 – 1968</u>,
he was the father of these four children:

1. <u>Mary Lourdes Grabenstein</u> (1922 - 2016)
2. <u>Martha Veronica Grabenstein</u> (1924 - 1930)
3. <u>William J. Grabenstein</u> (1926 - 1987)
4. <u>Robert James Grabenstein</u> (1931 - 2007)

From the *Cumberland Evening Times* Obituary of Wednesday, November 29, 1961, and from his Draft Card and parish records, I was able to gain these facts about Peter H. Grabenstein:

1. Peter was born April 17, 1889.
2. He was a member of St. Michael's Parish in Frostburg.
3. In 1942, at the age of 53, he registered for the WWII Draft, at which time he was a dairy farmer in the Winchester Bridge area, stood 5'6" tall, weighed 160lbs, had a fair complexion, brown hair, and blue eyes.
4. He was 72 years old when he died.
5. He was a retired dairyman when he died.
6. He was a lifelong resident of Winchester Road.
7. He died Tuesday, November 28, 1961.
8. He died at Sacred Heart Hospital, where he had been a patient for a week.
9. He was survived by his widow, <u>Delores Leah *Metzner* Grabenstein 1889 - 1968</u>
10. He was survived by a daughter: <u>Mary L. Grabenstein</u>, at home.
11. His 6-year-old daughter <u>Martha Veronica</u> died in 1930.
12. He was survived by two sons: <u>William J. Grabenstein</u> of Frostburg, and <u>Robert J. Grabenstein</u>, with the Army in Bamberg, Germany at the time of Peter's death.
13. His Requiem Mass was celebrated at St. Michaels in Frostburg.
14. He is buried at St. Michaels Cemetery.

"P.H. Grabenstein"
His signature on his WWII Draft Registration Card
Signed April 22, 1942

I have been to this grave of Peter H. Grabenstein in St. Michael's Cemetery in Frostburg, where Peter is buried next to his wife, Delores Leah *Metzner* Grabenstein. Also buried nearby are two of their children: Mary Lourdes and Robert James. The little Martha Veronica is buried on the other side of the cemetery, Section C, next to Joseph Metzner. That accounts for all the graves of Peter's children except William, who was cremated.

Mary Lourdes Grabenstein 1922 - 2016
(Daughter of Peter Henry Grabenstein)

The 1930 *U.S. Census,* regarding the Winchester Road household of Peter Grabenstein, provides thus:

<u>Peter</u> Grabenstein, 40, Head of House / <u>Delores</u> 37, Wife
[Their son <u>Robert</u>, born 1931, was not born in time for this census]

<u>Mary Lourdes</u>, 7, Daughter
<u>Martha Veronica</u>, 6, Daughter
<u>William J</u>, 3, Son
<u>Ella</u> Metzner, 42, Sister-in-Law

I have been to the Grave of Mary Lourdes Grabenstein in St. Michael's Cemetery in Frostburg, led there by a very helpful parish volunteer, Susan Gerhard of the office staff, who knew Mary Lourdes very well. Mary Lourdes had been a member of St. Michael's choir.

The *Rosary Basilica* in Lourdes, France

"Lourdes," pronounced "Lurd" in French and "Lurdz" in English, was never a very popular name for girls. Even at the height of its popularity, there were not many parents naming their baby girl "Lourdes." These Grabensteins, however, were very Catholic, and most good Catholics are familiar with the apparitions of the Blessed Virgin Mary at the village of Lourdes, France in the mid 1800's. *Our Lady of Lourdes* is a title of the Virgin in honor of the apparitions, so it is less surprising that a devout Catholic family would name their daughter after both the Virgin and the Apparitions. Hence, "Mary Lourdes."

Finally, in the <u>Saints Peter & Paul Yearbook of 1941</u>, we get to put a face of considerable character to the elegant name of Mary Lourdes:

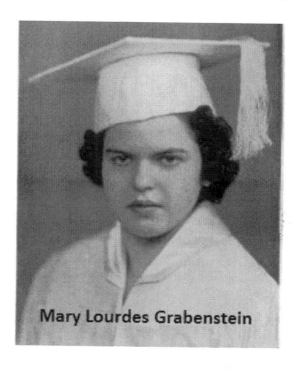

Born August 7, 1922 - Died July 8, 2016

In addition to being the Class Vice President when the Mass was still celebrated in Latin, Mary Lourdes was a member of the Latin Club, the French Club, the Glee Club, and the St. Agnes Mission Unit.

Requiescat in Pace

Mary Lourdes Grabenstein was only eight years old when her little sister Martha died in 1930.

Martha Veronica Grabenstein 1924 - 1930
(Daughter of Peter Henry Grabenstein)

Peter Grabenstein's other daughter at the 1930 census, according to census takers, was Martha Veronica, who died just nine days after the census taker visited the Grabenstein home.

She was 6 years old.

I located the grave of Martha Veronica at St. Michael's Cemetery in Frostburg, where she is buried in the Metzner lot, immediately beside her mother's brother, Joseph H. Metzner, in Section C just off of Mount Pleasant Street. Her humble little stone is quite weathered and barely legible, yet I could read on the face of it "Martha V. Grabenstein," and the top of it is inscribed with the now nearly-indiscernible endearment of "Our Darling."

Martha was counted in the census on April 23 of 1930. Nine days later, on May 2, 1930, she died at the age of 6.

I found two newspaper articles regarding the death of little Martha Veronica Grabenstein. I will present the May 5 obituary here. The May 6 obituary, also in the *Cumberland Evening Times*, states that Martha was a student in St. Michael's School, that she was a favorite among her classmates, that she died at home, and that the sadness of her early death, along with her apparent popularity with other children, resulted in a very large and touching funeral.

Cumberland Evening Times, May 5, 1930

Funeral of Child

"The funeral of Martha Grabenstein, age 6, daughter of Mr. and Mrs. P.H. Grabenstein, Winchester Bridge, who died Friday, was held at Saint Michaels Church, Frostburg, at 9:30 o'clock this morning. Rev. William J. McVeigh was celebrant at the Holy Angel's Mass.

The children of Saint Michael's School formed a bodyguard from the gate to the church. As the funeral procession entered the church, Rev. Father Nolan sang "Mother of God" and "Ave Maria" at the offertory.

Father Nolan preached a sermon at the end of Mass, "Suffer Little Children to Come Unto Me, For Such is The Kingdom of Heaven." As the body was carried out the school, children sang "Sweet Saviour, Bless Us Ere We Go."

The flower carriers were chosen from her classmates. The pallbearers were: DeSales Grabenstein, Richard Grabenstein, John Boyle, and Estel Brown.

In the Sanctuary were: Rev. Father Pius, SS Peter & Paul Monastery; Father Weber, Frostburg, and Rev. Father Bradley, Saint Mary's, Lonaconing."

William J. Grabenstein 1926 - 1987
(Son of Peter Henry Grabenstein)

Cumberland Times/News, July 8, 1987

"FROSTBURG - William J. Grabenstein, 60, of 78 Mount Pleasant Street, died Tuesday in Sacred Heart Hospital in Cumberland.

Born in Cumberland August 29, 1926, he was the son of the late Peter H. and Delores *Metzner* Grabenstein.

A member of St. Michael's Catholic Church, he was a graduate of LaSalle High School and the University of Maryland. Mr. Grabenstein served in the Army's 3rd Armored Division in the European theater during WWII. He was a member of Farrady Post 24, American Legion; Old Rail Post 6025, VFW, Mount Savage; Moose Lodge 271, Cumberland; Cumberland Knights of Columbus; and Haystack Mountain Sportsmen's Club.

Surviving are his widow, Helen C. *McCormick* Grabenstein; one son, William M. Grabenstein, at home; one sister, Miss Mary Lourdes Grabenstein, Winchester Road; one brother, Robert J. Grabenstein, Frostburg; and several nieces and nephews.

The body will be cremated, and a memorial service will be held at a later date. The Sowers Funeral Home is in charge of arrangements."

William and his brother Robert both had been pallbearers in 1973 for their aunt Nellie *Grabenstein* Barton.

The Social Security Death Index recorded William's official date of death as July 7, 1987.

According to U.S. Phone and Address Directories, William lived in Frostburg at 78 Mt. Pleasant Street, the street that passes St. Michel's Cemetery, where lies his father, mother, sisters Mary Lourdes and Martha Veronica, and brother Robert.

Robert James Grabenstein 1931 - 2007
(Son of Peter Henry Grabenstein)

Cumberland Times-News, June 4, 2007

"Born April 7, 1931 in Cumberland, he was the son of the late Peter and Delores Grabenstein. In addition to his parents, he was preceded in death by one brother, William; one sister, Martha, and his wife, Ruth Virginia *McCormick* Grabenstein.

Mr. Grabenstein was a retired Master Sergeant of the U.S. Army and later retired from the Maryland State Highway Administration. He served two tours in Vietnam, the first as an American advisor and the second with the 4th Infantry Division….

Surviving are one daughter, Linda McKenzie; one son, Robert Grabenstein; one granddaughter, Laura McKenzie; all of Frostburg; one sister, Mary L. Grabenstein of LaVale; a sister-in-law, Dorothy Yarnall and husband Jack of Cumberland; a brother-in-law, Charles McCormick and wife Corine of Florida, and numerous nieces and nephews.

A Funeral Mass will be celebrated at St. Michael's Catholic Church on Tuesday at 10 a.m. with Father James Hannon as celebrant'.

Interment will be at St. Michael's Cemetery.

Military Honors will be accorded at the graveside by members of the Vietnam Veterans of America 172."

Elizabeth Mary *Grabenstein* McKenzie 1893 - 1961
(Daughter of Mary Catherine *Martz* Grabenstein)

The 1930 *U.S. Census* declares Julius Grabenstein, age 72, a widower, the farmer we know to have been the husband of Mary Catherine *Martz* Grabenstein, to have the following individuals living in his home at the time of the census:

>Elizabeth McKenzie, a daughter, age 37
>William E. McKenzie, son-in-law, age 34

We might imagine that Julius, who lost his wife when he was 64, was now a 72-year-old man who had suffered the wear of many years on the farm and the railroad, and who now benefited from having his daughter and her husband in the house with him. Unfortunately, however, that arrangement ended soon after the census was taken, for Julius died September 23, 1930.

Nine years later, William E. McKenzie was dead, and Elizabeth was a patient in a Baltimore hospital:

>William Ellis McKenzie
>(Husband of Elizabeth *Grabenstein* McKenzie)

Cumberland Evening Times, June 28, 1939

"Funeral services for William Ellis McKenzie, 44, Cresaptown, who died Saturday night, June 24, at Allegany Hospital, were conducted this morning at St. Joseph's Catholic Church. Interment was in Belvedere Cemetery in Midland. A son of Leo McKenzie, Gilmore, he was a World War Veteran….Besides his father, he is survived by his wife, the former Miss Elizabeth Grabenstein of Cresaptown, a patient in a Baltimore Hospital."

THE MARTZ CONNECTION

Cumberland Evening Times, December 29, 1961:

"Mrs. Elizabeth Mary McKenzie, 70, former resident, died yesterday in Springfield State Hospital [Sykesville].

A native of Allegany County, she was a daughter of Julius and Mary *Martz* Grabenstein. Her husband, William McKenzie, died in 1939. Mrs. McKenzie was a former member of Saint Ambrose Catholic Church.

She is survived by a brother, Bernard Grabenstein, Chestertown, and two sisters, Mrs. Russell Winters, Cresaptown, and Mrs. Harmon Barton, McMullen Highway.

The body will be returned to the George Funeral Home."

The above obituary does not tell us where Elizabeth is buried, but I was able to find her grave by searching the parish records at *Our Lady of The Mountains* Catholic parish in Cumberland, where I discovered her to be buried at SS Peter & Paul Cemetery, in an unmarked grave in the same plot with her mother, father, sister Anna, and an "Infant Grabenstein" who was stillborn and buried there February 6, 1932.

Twelve Graves in This Grabenstein Plot

Springfield State Hospital, Sykesville, MD

The Last Home of Elizabeth *Grabenstein* McKenzie, Daughter of Julius and Mary Catherine *Martz* Grabenstein

By the late 1940's and 1950's, the hospital population exceeded 3000. Units were overcrowded, and staffing was inadequate to meet the needs of the patients. A series of newspaper articles in the *Baltimore Sun*, entitled "Maryland's Shame," examined these problems at all the state operated psychiatric hospitals. As a result of these articles and heightened awareness by the public of the needs of the mentally ill, additional funding for staffing and capital improvements was made by the Maryland legislature. At Springfield Hospital Center, this effort resulted in the construction of many new buildings, and renovations to all existing buildings to remedy the overcrowding.

Herman Joseph Grabenstein 1893 - 1960

(Son of Mary Catherine *Martz* Grabenstein)

Cumberland Evening Times, July 11, 1960:

Herman J. Grabenstein

"Herman Joseph Grabenstein Sr., 66, of 604 Greene Street died yesterday at Sacred Heart Hospital. He had been in ill health for some time.

A native of Allegany County, Mr. Grabenstein was a son of Julius and Mary *Martz* Grabenstein.

Mr. Grabenstein retired from the Cumberland Post Office in August 1958 after 40 years of service. He began in 1918 as a substitute carrier in Frostburg and became a regular carrier in 1920. For many years he was a parcel post carrier and for five years prior to his retirement was a clerk at the Post Office.

He was a member of St. Patrick's Catholic Church and the Holy Name Society of the church. He also was a member of Cumberland Council 586 of Columbus and the National Association of Letter Carriers.

He is survived by his widow Mary *Greene* Grabenstein; two sons, Herman J. Grabenstein Jr., this city, and Thomas A. Grabenstein, Buffalo, N.Y.; two brothers, Bernard F. Grabenstein, Bowling Greene, and Peter Grabenstein, Winchester Road; three sisters, Mrs. Russell [Wressell] Winters, Cresaptown, Mrs. Harman Barton, McMullen Highway, and Elizabeth McKenzie, Baltimore, and nine grandchildren.

Requiem Mass will be celebrated on Wednesday at 9 a.m. in St. Patrick's Catholic Church, and interment will be in SS Peter & Paul Cemetery."

Herman had a son to whom he gave his name, and that was Herman Joseph Grabenstein Jr., who became a very accomplished man, and who became quite popular in Cumberland:

Herman Joseph Grabenstein Jr. 1921 - 2006

Deacon Grabenstein

Cumberland Times-News, June 22, 2006:

"Herman Joseph Grabenstein Jr., 85, of Cumberland, died Wednesday, June 21, 2006, at his home.

Born April 22, 1921, in Cumberland, he was the son of the late Herman J. and Mary (Greene) Grabenstein. He was preceded in death by one brother, Thomas A. Grabenstein; one brother-in-law, Dr. Leo H. Ley; and one sister-in-law, Lucille (Ley) Moser.

Mr. Grabenstein was a graduate of LaSalle High School, Class of 1939, and Catherman's Business School. He was a veteran of World War II, rank of first lieutenant in Army Air Force, served as flight engineer on B-29 Superfortress planes in the Pacific Theater and received Air Medal with four clusters, Purple Heart, and Distinguished Flying Cross with one cluster. Following his tour of military duty, he was employed at Spear's Jewelry Store and 35 years at S. T. Little Jewelry Company, where he was assistant manager and graduate of the Gemological Institute of America. Upon retirement in 1986, he was self-employed as a jewelry appraiser and in 1996 associated with J. Kreiger, Goldsmith, as a jewelry appraiser in the Kreiger business on North Mechanic Street.

He was a member of SS Peter & Paul Catholic Church, where he was ordained as deacon in the Archdiocese of Baltimore in October of 1976 by the late Bishop P. Francis Murphy. In 1994, along with his wife, Irene, he received the Archdiocesan Medal of Honor through his parish. In February of 2000, Herman was the recipient of the "Pro Ecclesia et Pontifice" (for Church and Pope) papal medal of honor, given to him by Pope John Paul II in recognition of outstanding service, and presented by William Cardinal Keeler, Archbishop of Baltimore, in a ceremony at the Basilica of Mary Our Queen in Baltimore. He was past grand commander and chaplain of Wamba Caravan 89, Order of the Alhambra; former treasurer of the Thomas B. Finan Auxiliary; life member of Council 586 Knights of Columbus; officer of the St. Vincent DePaul Society of his parish; and volunteered at St. Anthony Place Food Pantry of SS Peter & Paul Church.

Surviving are his wife, Irene (Ley) Grabenstein, whom he married Aug. 16, 1945; four children, Lawrence A. Grabenstein and wife Cheryl, Silver Spring, Brother Joseph L. Grabenstein, F.S.C., LaSalle University, Philadelphia, Pa., Jane Ellen Grabenstein, Pittsburgh, and Col. John D. Grabenstein, U.S. Army, and wife Laurie, Burke, Va.; grandchildren, Allison (Grabenstein) Oliver and husband Frank, Annapolis; Michael L. Grabenstein, Rockville; Emily, Andrea, Erica and Peter Grabenstein, all of Burke, Kara Kernus, Virginia Beach, and Jenna Kernus, Silver Spring; great-grandchildren, Taylor, Jacob and Peyton Oliver, all of Annapolis; sisters-in-law, Christine Grabenstein, St. Petersburg, Fla., Dorothy (Ley) Altice and Alberta (Ley) Robinson, both of Cumberland, and Mary Catherine (Ley) Kennedy, Daytona Beach; and brother-in-law, Robert G. Ley, Marietta, Ohio.

A Mass of Christian Burial will be celebrated at SS Peter & Paul Catholic Church Saturday at 11 a.m. with Father Bernard Finerty, O.F.M., Cap., and Father James Kurtz, O.F.M., Cap., as celebrants. Deacon Charles Hiebler, Archdiocese of Baltimore, will serve as deacon for the liturgy.

Interment will be in SS Peter & Paul Cemetery. Graveside military honors will be accorded by the Combined Veterans Honor Guard.

Honorary pallbearers will be Jim Kreiger, Thomas E. McConnell, Albert E. Brant, James E. Coyle, Thomas E. Carroll, J. Edward McMahon, Robert E. Carey, Michael P. Blake, Hon. Paul J. Stakem, Thomas J. Connelley, Edward P. Mullaney, William Datum, John J. Coyle, Brother Eric Henderson, F.S.C., Brother Herman Paul, F.S.C., Brother James Kirkpatrick, F.S.C., James A. Collins and William Blake."

Herman Joseph Grabenstein Sr. had also another son, who, unlike his brother, did not remain in the Cumberland area:

Thomas Aloysius Grabenstein 1923 - 2002

On July 28, 1949, Thomas Grabenstein, age 26, and Christine Lemonopoulos, age 22, who was born in Canton, Ohio, applied for a marriage license in Cleveland, Ohio. At that time, Thomas was a student, and Christine was a nurse. They married and remained married until his death in Florida in 2002.

Cumberland Times-News, June 19, 2002:

"SAINT PETERSBURG, Fla. – Thomas A. Grabenstein, 79, of St. Petersburg died Monday, June 17, 2002 at his residence.

Born in Cumberland, he came to Florida in 1982 from Chattanooga, Tennessee.

He was a graduate of Case Western Reserve, and received his MBA from State University of New York. He was a chemical engineer for DuPont for 32 years. An Army veteran of World War II, he fought in the Battle of The Bulge. He was a member of the Cathedral of Saint Jude The Apostle, the Knights of Columbus 5737, the Loyal Order of Moose 1145, the Suncoast Model Railroaders Club, and the DuPont Retirees.

He is survived by his wife of 52 years, Christine L.; five sons, Dr. Thomas G. and Dr. William P., both of Clarksville, Tenn., Dr. Jeffrey J., Oakridge, Tenn., Christopher, New York, N.Y., and Stephen J., Ashville, N.C.; a brother, Herman J., Cumberland; and 10 grandchildren."

Bernard Edward Grabenstein 1895 - 1966

(Son of Mary Catherine *Martz* Grabenstein)

Cumberland Evening Times, June 6, 1919:

Returned Soldier Honored

"Mr. and Mrs. Julius Grabenstein, near Winchester Bridge, last night entertained in honor of their son, Bernard, who returned from France a few weeks ago. Those present were: Mr. and Mrs. Wm. Lewis, Marshall and Pearl Porter, Joseph Grabenstein, Dora Lewis, Clara and Lucy Martz, Elza and Edward Lewis, Mary Margaret Vocke, Margaret Yates, Ralph Martz, Mary and Frances Boch, Joseph and Marie Metzner, Bernard Boch, Charles Martz, Lucy Grabenstein, Margaret and May Naughton, Anna and Clara Schaaf, Clara and Dora Reith, Regina Brant, Minnie and Bert Mertzfelt, Catherine Grabenstein, Michael Naughton, and Kirk Brantz and Charles Friend, of McKeesport.

A dance was held on the barn floor. The home was beautifully decorated.

Mr. Grabenstein left with the second draft from Frostburg, November 5, 1917 and was in service with Co. A, 15th Engineers over in France."

FADLEY

Bernard

From the *Cumberland Times News* Obituary, Wednesday, June 8, 1966:

1. He was 70 years old.
2. He was a retired machinist with the B&O Railroad in Cumberland.
3. He died June 7, 1966 in Ann Arundel General Hospital in Annapolis.
4. He had been ill three weeks and living with a son.
5. He was a member of Henry Hart Post 1411 VFW.
6. He was survived by his widow, Marie Helen *Elliot* Grabenstein.
7. He was survived by two sons:
   Anthony Grabenstein, Annapolis, Maryland
   Leroy Grayson, Salt Lake City, Utah
8. He was survived by two daughters:
   M. Kathleen Kerns, Landover Mills, Maryland
   Rose Marie Smool, Seabrook, Maryland
9. His Requiem Mass was celebrated at SS Peter & Paul in Cumberland.
10. He is buried at SS Peter & Paul Cemetery.

His draft registration card reports he lived in Bowling Green, was 5'6" tall, weighed 190 pounds, and had gray hair and hazel eyes and a sallow complexion.

Bernard E. Grabenstein
(Registrant's signature)

From his WWII Draft Registration Card
signed April 27, 1942

Nellie C. *Grabenstein* Barton 1898 - 1973

(Daughter of Mary Catherine *Martz* Grabenstein)

From visiting her grave:

1. Nellie was born April 17, 1898.
2. She died February 28, 1973.
3. Her husband was <u>Harmon J. Barton 1896 - 1978.</u>
4. She and Harmon are buried at St. Ambrose in Cresaptown.

Cumberland News, March 1, 1973:

Mrs. Harmon J. Barton

"Mrs. Nellie C. Barton, 74, of RD 6, McMullen Highway, died yesterday at Sacred Heart Hospital, shortly after being admitted. She had been in failing health several months.

Born in Cumberland, she was the daughter of the late Julius and Mary *Martz* Grabenstein.

She was a member of St. Ambrose Catholic Church, Christian Mothers, and Ladies Club of the church.

Surviving are her husband, Harmon J. Barton; two daughters, Mrs. John McDonald, Cumberland, and Mrs. Jean Umstot, RD 6, Cumberland; one son, H. Edward Barton, RD 6, Cumberland; eight grandchildren, and a number of nieces and nephews.

The body is at George Funeral Home where friends will be received from 2 to 4 and 7 to 9 p.m.

Mass of The Resurrection will be celebrated tomorrow at 10 a.m. at St. Ambrose Catholic Church. Interment will be in the parish cemetery.

Pallbearers will be Thomas J. Barton, Michael W. Skelley, William Grabenstein, Robert Grabenstein, and Floyd Smith."

II

JOHANNES

Johannes Martz 1858 - 1890
(Son of Peter and Alice Martz)

Buried at SS Peter and Paul Cemetery in Cumberland, he is the husband of Mary E. *Hart* Martz 1867 - 1934 with whom he had at least two children:

Lucy Martz 1887 - 1894
and
John W. Martz 1889 - 1920

At age 3, Johannes survived the *Attack on The 21st Bridge* in 1861 during the "War Between The States," the U.S. Civil War.

Johannes was born in, and died in, Allegany County, Maryland. He was born on February 24, 1858, and he died at the age of 32 on May 18, 1890. Well before his death, Johannes had become known by the anglicized name of "John," and his gravestone bears the name of "John." He also named his son "John."

1981 Re-issue of 1858 Certificate

Certificate of Baptism

Ss. Peter & Paul Church
125 FAYETTE STREET
CUMBERLAND, MARYLAND 21502

This is to Certify

That __John (Maerz) Martz__

Child of __Peter Maerz__

and __Margaretha Wigger__

born in __Willer Creek__ (CITY) _____ (STATE)

on the __14__ day of __February__ A.D. __1858__

was **Baptized**

on the __14__ day of __March__ A.D. __1858__

According to the Rite of the Roman Catholic Church by the Rev. __VandeBraak__

the Sponsors being { __John Furster__ }

as appears from the Baptismal Register of this Church.

Dated __7/15/81__

Pastor

Cumberland Daily Times, May 19, 1890

DIED YESTERDAY

"John Martz, aged 32 years, died at 11 o'clock yesterday morning of heart failure at the residence of his brother on Hickory Alley. The funeral will take place tomorrow morning at 9 o'clock from SS Peter & Paul Church."

When Johannes died in 1890, his bereft widow was only twenty-three. His little John was but a baby, and his little Lucy was only 3 years old. Lucy would live only a few years after her father's death, for she would die at the age of 7, and little John lived only to the age of 31.

The top face of his simple-but-sturdy stone proclaims "Father" and the unfortunately truncated lifespan of "1858 - 1890."

Less visible in this photo is the inscription in the shadow on the front face, simply "John Martz," a testimony to his having accepted the anglicized version of his name, but the top face seems to bear that which he might have considered his greatest role in life: "Father."

Johannes' Wife

Mary E. *Hart* Martz

Although I found very little about Johannes' wife, Mary *Hart* Martz, we can feel the sorrow of this young woman who in 1890, at the age of 23, with a baby and a 3-year-old, suffered the death of her husband, and who only four years later suffered the death of her 7-year-old little girl, and who eventually would have to bury her only other child.

Barely visible in the shadow on the front of this stone is the name of Mary Martz, the mother bereft of husband and children:

These precious few facts are all I could thus far recover from the short life of Johannes Martz and his wife, and the following is all I have regarding his children who, like their father, were allotted but a short stay among the living:

THE MARTZ CONNECTION

When Mary *Hart* Martz buried her husband Johannes in SS Peter & Paul Cemetery in 1890, she had her three-year-old Lucy and baby John to care for. She did not, however, remarry. Instead, at least as early as the 1900 census, after she had lost Lucy at the age of 7 in 1894, Mary and her remaining child, John, moved back into her parents' house. Those parents were Peter and Elizabeth Eva Hart, and they lived on Mechanic Street in Cumberland. Mr. Hart was a grocer, as the censuses list him as manager of a grocery store.

At the 1900 census, Mary Hart Martz and John, age 10, lived at the Hart residence, and John was listed as attending school.

At the 1910 census, Mary and son John, age 20, were still at the Hart residence, and John was still single.

At the 1920 census, Mary, 52, and John, now 30, were still at the same Mechanic Street address, and John was still single. The census was taken in January 1920, and John died later that year at the age of 31, having lived virtually his entire life in the home of his grandparents, the Harts.

At the 1930 census, Mary, 62, was still at the Mechanic street home of her parents, but those parents are not listed in the home at that census, so presumably they had passed away, while Mary remained in the home with her sisters, Cecelia, 47, and Louise, 45. Cecelia was listed as the Head of House, and her occupation as "saleslady in a grocery store." Recall that Mr. Hart had been a grocer.

This 1930 census, of course, would be the last census that would count Mary *Hart* Martz, for she would die in 1934 after having to bury her husband and her only two children.

The Children of Johannes Martz:

Lucy Martz 1887 - 1894
(Daughter of Johannes Martz)

1. She was about 7 years old.
2. She was born in 1887.
3. She was only 3 years old when her father died.
4. She lived without a father only 4 more years, for she died in 1894 at the age of 7.
5. She is buried at SS Peter & Paul Cemetery in Cumberland.

Barely legible in the shadow on the front face of this stone is the name of Lucy Martz

John W. Martz 1889 - 1920

(Son of Johannes Martz)

1. He was about 31 years old.
2. He was born in 1889.
3. He was but a baby when his father died in 1890.
4. A few years after his father's death, he was only 5 years old when his 7-year-old sister died.
5. He himself died in 1920 at the age of only 31.
6. After the deaths of his father and sister, he and his mother went to live the remainder of their lives in the home of her parents, the Harts.
7. He is buried at SS Peter & Paul Cemetery in Cumberland.

Barely visible in the shadow on the front of this stone
is the name of John W. Martz

III

ANNA CATHERINE

Anna Catherine *Martz* Boch 1860 - 1919
(Daughter of Peter and Alice Martz)

Born in February of 1860, Anna died of heart and lung ailments at the age of 58 on January 10, 1919. She was buried on January 14, 1919 at SS Peter & Paul Cemetery in Cumberland.

Anna is the wife of <u>Joseph Boch 1850 - 1901</u>. Joseph, a farmer first in Cash Valley and then in Ellerslie, was born in Maryland after his parents, John and Catherine, immigrated from Darmstadt, Germany.

Joseph and Anna had nine children:

John Julius Boch 1884 - 1962
George Henry Boch 1886 - 1943
Catherine Elizabeth *Boch* McKenzie 1888 - 1970
Agnes Ann Boch 1891 - 1900
Anna Elizabeth Boch 1893 - 1901
Bernard Joseph Boch 1896 - 1973
Mary Barbara *Boch* Condon 1896 - 1945
Frances Cecelia *Boch* Grabenstein 1898 - 1980
Joseph Edward Boch 1900 - 1901

1981 Re-issue of 1860 Certificate

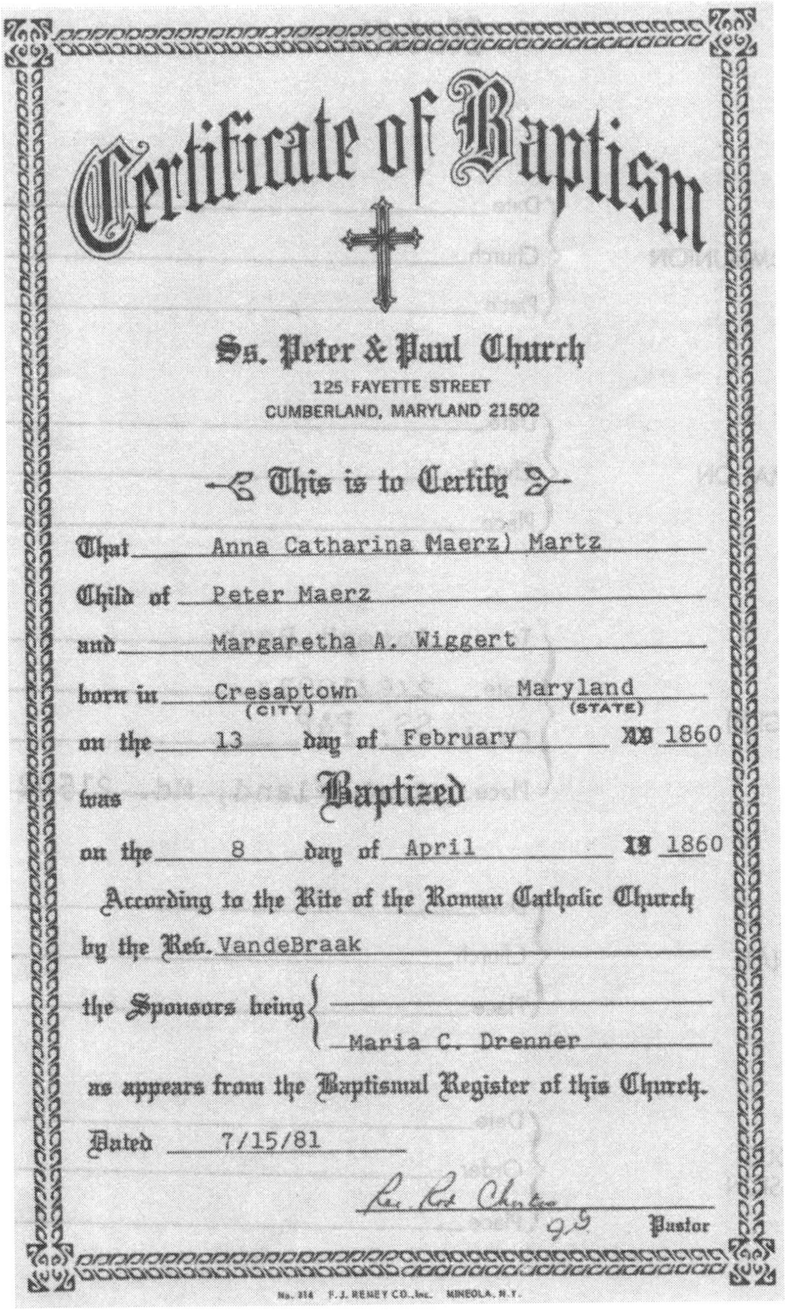

Certificate of Baptism

Ss. Peter & Paul Church
125 FAYETTE STREET
CUMBERLAND, MARYLAND 21502

This is to Certify

That Anna Catharina Maerz) Martz

Child of Peter Maerz

and Margaretha A. Wiggert

born in Cresaptown (CITY) Maryland (STATE)

on the 13 day of February A.D. 1860

was **Baptized**

on the 8 day of April 19 1860

According to the Rite of the Roman Catholic Church

by the Rev. VandeBraak

the Sponsors being {
Maria C. Drenner

as appears from the Baptismal Register of this Church.

Dated 7/15/81

Pastor

No. 314 F.J. REMEY CO., Inc. MINEOLA, N.Y.

Anna Catherine *Martz* was the youngest survivor of the *Attack on The 21st Bridge* in 1861 during the U.S. Civil War, when she was a baby in her daddy's arms as he crawled with her through a grain field, while bullets whistled and whizzed overhead. This inauspicious beginning to Anna's life was followed by an adulthood of considerable sorrow, for in the year 1900 she would suffer the death of her nine-year old child, little Agnes, and in the following year, 1901, she would endure the deaths of her husband, eight-year-old Ann, and baby Joseph.

The above are images of two different sides of the same stone at SS Peter & Paul Cemetery, a stone that on one side (pictured left) marks the burial place of <u>Joseph</u> and <u>Anna C. *Martz* Boch</u>, while the adjacent side of the same stone (right) marks the burial place of three of their children: <u>Agnes, 9</u>, <u>Anna, 8</u>, and <u>Joseph, infant</u>. Upon the death of Anna C. in 1919, she had been preceded in death only by her husband and these three children.

The Children of Anna Catherine *Martz* Boch:

John Julius Boch 1884 - 1962

(Son of Anna Catherine *Martz* Boch)

From the *Cumberland Sunday Times,* Obituary, Sunday, April 8, 1962:

1. He was 77 years old.
2. He retired from *The Cumberland Brewing Company* in about 1956.
3. On April 7, 1962, he died suddenly at home in Baltimore, where he had been living since his retirement from the *Cumberland Brewing Company* six years earlier.
4. He was survived by his wife, Clara *Helbig* Boch, formerly of Mt. Savage.
5. He was survived by one son:
   Edward Boch, Kensington, Maryland
6. He was survived by five daughters:
   Mildred *Boch* Brant, Rantoll, Illinois
   Rita *Boch* Crouse, Arlington, Virginia
   Carol Boch, Washington
   Marion Boch, Washington
   Helen Boch, at home
7. His Requiem Mass was celebrated at St. Dominic Catholic Church in Baltimore.
8. He is buried in Wheaton, Maryland.

John Julius Boch worked at the same brewery as did his uncle Johannes Bernhart Martz, as well as his cousin Francis J. Martz. The three of them, that is, retired from the *Cumberland Brewing Company*.

As beer is a major part of German culture, this writer, beer-drinker, and relative of these brewers feels a peculiar sense of pride in these German kin who were able to participate in the production of this popular beverage so important to the culture of their ancestors.

John Boch is pictured above with two of his uncles.

LEFT TO RIGHT:

John Metzner   John Julius Boch   Peter Martin Martz

Notice in the above photo, in the rail cart, the handle of an old wooden coal scoop, a poignant symbol of the black gold that pulsed through the veins of Appalachia, creating jobs in the mines, heating the homes, giving life to industry and the railroads, and providing a livelihood for so many.

George Henry Boch 1886 - 1943

(Son of Anna Catherine *Martz* Boch)

From newspaper archives, the *U.S. Census*, and his WWII Draft Card, I found the following about George Henry Boch:

1. He was born in Allegany County, and he died in Allegany County at the age of 56.
2. He was born on September 9, 1886 and died March 19, 1943.
3. His wife was Frances R. *Burkey* Boch.
4. He had a tattoo of a cross on his right upper arm.

L to R: Catherine Elizabeth *Boch* McKenzie, George Henry Boch, and Frances Cecilia *Martz* McBee

Cumberland Evening Times
March 19, 1943

"George Henry Boch, 56, of LaVale, died suddenly this morning. A track foreman for the Western Maryland Railway, Mr. Boch went to work this morning but returned home because he was not feeling well. He was a native of Corriganville, the son of Joseph and Anna *Martz* Boch. Survivors include his wife, Mrs. Frances *Burkey* Boch; five sons, George A., Joseph J., Richard A., and Paul L. Boch, all of LaVale, and Vincent B. Boch, U.S. Army, Pearl Harbor, Hawaii; two daughters, Sister Mary Urban, member of the Ursuline order in Morgantown, West Virginia, and Mrs. John A. Fishell, LaVale; two brothers, John Boch, LaVale, and Bernard Boch, Washington, D.C.; and three sisters, Mrs. Catherine McKenzie, Mrs. Frances Grabenstein, and Mrs. Mary Condon, all of LaVale. Mr. Boch was a member of SS Peter & Paul Catholic Church and the parish Holy Name Society."

The Children of George Henry Boch:

Based on the total *U.S. Census* record regarding the household of George Henry Boch in both the 1930 and 1940 censuses, I will hereby commit to the following list of <u>seven</u> children born to George H. Boch:

1. Mary Teresa Boch 1915 - 1961
2. Ruth Margaret *Boch* Fishell 1917 - 1962
3. George Ambrose Boch 1919 - 1999
4. Joseph Jerome Boch 1921 - 1996
5. Vincent Bernard Boch 1923 - 2005
6. Richard Anthony Boch 1928 - 2017
7. Paul Leo Boch 1930 - 2005

Mary Teresa Boch 1915 - 1961
(Daughter of George Henry Boch)

Mary Teresa Becomes Mary Urban:

At a very young age, George's first-born daughter, Mary Teresa, left the family home to become a nun, and she joined the Catholic Church's *Congregation of The Ursulines* and began her life of devotion to God with the *Ursuline Sisters of Louisville,* in Louisville, Kentucky.

In the Catholic tradition, as well as in many other religious and cultural traditions, the taking of a new name is symbolic of entering into a new place in one's life. Mary Teresa took the name of "Mary Urban." The name "Urban" might sound strange to the non-Catholic reader, but Catholics know of several popes who took that same name.

After a life of service to others, the body of Sister Mary Urban Boch is laid to rest at plot 256 at St. Michael Cemetery in Louisville, Kentucky.

Her Stone
St. Michael Cemetery in Louisville, Kentucky

The Chapel at The Ursuline Sisters' Motherhouse in Louisville
(Where Sister Mary Urban Lived, Worshiped, and Prayed)

Since 1917, the chapel has been a sacred space for the Ursuline Sisters. It is the place where they worship daily, where they come together for special celebrations, and where they made vows to God and commitments to each other. The chapel is holy ground where they are strengthened and renewed to carry Christ to others by the witness of their lives, and where they share their deep value of prayer.

<u>Sister Mary Urban Boch</u>
<u>May 2, 1915 - November 3, 1961</u>
(Mary Teresa Boch)

Daughter of George Henry Boch,
Granddaughter of Anna Catherine *Martz* Boch

How proud Peter and Alice Martz would have been
to know their great-granddaughter was a nun.

Sister Mary Urban Boch

Cumberland Evening Times, November 3, 1961

"Sister Mary Urban Boch, a member of the Ursuline Order of nuns, died this morning at the Ursuline Mother House in Louisville, Kentucky, following an illness of 11 months.

A daughter of Frances R. Boch, National Highway, and the late George H. Boch, she had been a member of the religious order 29 years. She was Principal and Superior of Holy Spirit School in Louisville.

Sister Mary Urban received a bachelor of arts degree from Ursuline College and a master's degree from Creighton University. During her teaching career, she taught at Morgantown, West Virginia, North Platte, Nebraska, and numerous schools in the Louisville area.

Surviving, besides her mother, are five brothers, George A. Boch, this city, Joseph J. Boch, Maple Heights, Ohio, Vincent B. Boch, Bel Air, Richard A. Boch, Pittsburgh, and Paul L. Boch, LaVale; and a sister, Mrs. John A. Fishell, city.

A Requiem Mass will be celebrated Monday at 9 a.m. at the Ursuline Mother House Chapel, 3115 Lexington Road, Louisville, and interment will be in St. Michael's Cemetery there.

The family requests that memorials be in the form of masses."

Holy Spirit School in Louisville, Kentucky,
Where Sister Mary Urban Boch Was Principal

Catherine Elizabeth *Boch* McKenzie 1888 - 1970

(Daughter of Anna Catherine *Martz* Boch)

From *Cumberland Times,* Obituary on December 30, 1970:

1. She was born in Corriganville, Maryland.
2. She died at home at 307 Wills Creek Avenue.
3. She was the wife of Walter E. McKenzie 1882 - 1938.
4. She was a member of SS Peter & Paul in Cumberland.
5. She was survived by three sons:
    Ambrose R. McKenzie, Cumberland
    Paul M. McKenzie, Olney
    Leo E. McKenzie, Rockville
6. [Her son Michael preceded her in death in 1938.]
7. She was survived by five daughters:
    Regina Manley, Baltimore
    Margaret Strong, Westernport
    Helen Cessna, Silver Spring
    Catherine Kelly, Cumberland
    Bernadette Browning, Silver Spring
8. Catherine is buried in the SS Peter & Paul Cemetery.

The Children of Catherine Elizabeth *Boch* McKenzie:

Ambrose Raymond
1910 - 2003

Mary Regina
1912 - 1979

Michael Edward
1913 - 1938

Anna Margaret
1916 - 2011

Helen Frances
1919 - 2012

Catherine Ruth
1922 - 1988

Paul M.
1923 - 2010

Mary Bernadette
1926 - 2014

Leo E.
(Still living as of this publication)

Catherine Elizabeth *Boch* McKenzie

Agnes Ann Boch 1891 - 1900
(Daughter of Anna Catherine *Martz* Boch)

From the 1900 *U.S. Census:*

Born in January of 1891, Agnes was 9 years old and at home with her parents in Ellerslie, Maryland when the census was taken in that town on July 2, 1900.

From the inscription on her stone at SS Peter & Paul Cemetery, a stone she shares with her mother, father, sister Anna, and brother Joseph, we see that Agnes died in 1900, meaning she died at age 9.

Among the other preciously few facts we can learn from a census, we know that Agnes was in school and that she could read and write.

Anna Elizabeth Boch 1893 - 1901
(Daughter of Anna Catherine *Martz* Boch)

From the 1900 *U S. Census*:

Born in July of 1893, Anna was 6 years old and at home with her parents in Ellerslie, Maryland when the census was taken in that town July 2, 1900.

From the inscription on her stone at SS Peter & Paul Cemetery, a stone she shares with her mother, father, sister Agnes, and brother Joseph, we see that Anna died in 1901, at the age of 7 or 8.

From the census, we see that Anna was not yet in school, and we see that her family called her "Annie."

Bernard Joseph Boch 1896 - 1973

(Son of Anna Catherine *Martz* Boch)

Twin Brother of Mary Barbara Boch

A veteran of WWI, he registered again at age 46 for WWII:

His WWII Draft Registration Card:

[Draft Registration Card image showing:
- Serial Number: 504
- Name: Bernard Joseph Boch
- Place of Residence: 4302 Fessenden St. N.W. Wash. D.C.
- Mailing Address: Same
- Telephone: Em. 0983
- Age: 46
- Place of Birth: Corringuille, Maryland
- Date of Birth: 2-24-1896
- Name of Person Who Will Always Know Your Address: Percy Sattell - Undertaker - 1418 H St. N.W. Wash. D.C.
- Employer: Stanley Horner Corp.
- Place of Employment: Champlain St. N.W. - Wash. D.C.
- Signed: Bernard J. Boch]

From the *Cumberland Evening Times,* Obituary of August 21, 1973, and from his Draft Registration, we have the following regarding the life of Bernard Joseph Boch:

1. He was born in Maryland on February 24, 1896.
2. He was born with a twin sister, Mary Barbara *Boch* Condon.
3. His wife was Mary F. *McKenna* Boch 1899 - 1968.
4. He died at age 77 on August 18, 1973.
5. He is buried in SS Peter & Paul Cemetery in Cumberland.
6. At his funeral, the *Knights of Columbus* formed the honor guard.
7. His memorial stone proclaims: "PFC U.S. Army World War I."

Mary Barbara *Boch* Condon 1896 - 1945

(Daughter of Anna Catherine *Martz* Boch)

Twin Sister of Bernard Joseph Boch

From the *Cumberland Sunday Times* Obituary, December 16, 1945, we have the following regarding the life of Mary Barbara *Boch* Condon:

1. She was born in LaVale on February 24, 1896.
2. She was born with a twin brother, Bernard J. Boch.
3. She was the wife of William F. Condon 1888 – 1952.
4. She was a Registered Nurse.
5. She died at age 49 on December 15, 1945 in Allegany Hospital in Cumberland two hours after being admitted, having suffered a stroke.
6. She was survived by a daughter, Angela, of the home.
7. She was a member of the SS Peter & Paul Parish in Cumberland.
8. She is buried in the SS Peter & Paul Cemetery.

Only three months after seeing the end of WWII, Mary Barbara *Boch* Condon, herself a nurse, passed away in Allegany Hospital, which stood on Decatur Street in Cumberland. It was built as a 25-bed facility in 1905, but by 1913, two years after the Catholic Daughters of Charity took over the hospital administration, it had tripled in size, necessitating the addition of a five-story annex to the hospital in 1936.

The name Allegany Hospital changed to Sacred Heart Hospital in 1952, and it moved from Decatur Street to Seton Drive on Haystack Mountain in 1967.

Saint Elizabeth Ann Seton founded the first American congregation of religious sisters, the Daughters of Charity, perhaps a point of interest for many of Cumberland's citizens familiar with Seton Drive.

The Children of Anna Catherine *Martz* Boch:

Three (3) of Her Nine (9) Children:
Mary, Frances, and Bernard

Frances Cecelia *Boch* Grabenstein 1898 - 1980
(Daughter of Anna Catherine *Martz* Boch)

Cumberland Evening Times, March 19, 1980

"Mrs. Frances Cecelia Grabenstein, 81, Of 625 Elwood Street, died yesterday in Memorial Hospital.

Born May 5, 1898, in Cumberland, she was a daughter of the late Joseph Boch and Annie *Martz* Boch. Her husband, James E. Grabenstein died in April 1979.

She was a former employee of Peoples Drug Store and a retired seamstress. She was a member of St. Mary's Catholic Church, the Sodality, and the Senior Citizens and St. Mary's Elders.

Surviving are a son, James B. Grabenstein, this city; one daughter, Mrs. Josephine F. Robey, city; nine grandchildren and 15 great – grandchildren."   [Frances is buried in St. Mary's Cemetery.]

Frances was a member of St. Mary's in Cumberland.

Joseph Edward Boch 1900 - 1901
(Son of Anna Catherine *Martz* Boch)

Joseph is not listed in the home with his parents in Ellerslie when the census was taken in that town on July 2, 1900, most likely because he had not yet been born, so I surmise he was born in the second half of that year.

His stone in SS Peter & Paul Cemetery tells us he was born in 1900 and died in 1901, so we know he was but an infant, a little one perhaps whose only mark on earth is now fading away on a stone he shares with his mother, father, and sisters Agnes and Anna. Even as the stone reluctantly submits to Time, however, it is my earnest hope that this book will secure the fact of this child's existence, for it has been said that "no man is dead while his name is still spoken."

Anna Catherine *Martz* Boch
1860 - 1919

Though she had been only an infant and unable to remember losing her home to the attack on the 21st Bridge, Anna would live to feel the death of her little Agnes in 1900, and then the deaths of her husband, her little Anna, and baby Joseph all in 1901.

I imagine Anna to have been a very strong woman to bear the rapid succession of the deaths of her husband and three children, but I often wondered what she did after those terrible events, but my wondering was somewhat appeased when Anna's great-niece, Teresa Savage, provided me with a letter written by Anna's son John in 1901, after Anna apparently took her remaining six children and moved back into the old Matz place. I don't know to whom it was addressed, but John was Anna's oldest son and was about seventeen when he wrote this very enlightening, very touching letter, a letter apparently written from the old Matz Place:

Cresaptown, Md
Dec 14, 1901

Dear Friend,

I write to you to let you know that I am well, and I hope that you are the same, and I suppose you all live on the mountain yet.

I will let you know we do not live in Cash Valley now. We have moved up to Cresaptown, to our grampapa's house, about a mile and a half from Cresaptown. We moved about the first of September. We sold our cow and horse, and we moved all our straw up here, and we all live together here.

We butchered our hogs on the tenth of this month. We had two and Grampapa two, which made four, and we butchered an old cow on the second of the month, and we have a good lot of meat now for a while. We caught eight rabbits this fall, and we will try to get a couple more yet till New Year. We have not had much snow yet for to catch rabbits.

I do not get to Cumberland very much now since we live up here. I have not seen you since last fall. I did work on the Eckhart Railroad last spring for about three weeks, and, if things does not go right, I will try it again.

We are a going to clear some more ground this winter. We have made one hundred and fifty gallons of apple butter. We had a great many apples up here, and cherries too, and we made three barrels of sauerkraut and about five barrels of cider, and we do a great deal of marketing here. They have two horses and two cows and about fifty chickens and a great many dogs and cats.

We did not want to stay in Cash Valley. We could not find an empty house either, and they wanted us to come and live with them, and we are here now. We have a large house here as there are ten in the house now, seven of us and three of them: Gramfather and Garmmother and Aunt Fannie, which is home yet. And as it was raining very hard this afternoon, I thought I would write to you and let you know how we all are, and I send this letter to Corriganville, for I thought that some of yous would pass there and get it.

Address your letters to

                John Boch
                Cresaptown, Md

Goodbye.

                Your Friend,
                John Boch

        P.S.

I forgot to tell you that Miss Katie Martz got married on the 27 of November this year to a fellow in New York by the name of Erhardt Duffner.

IV

HEINRICH WILHELM

"HENRY"

Heinrich Wilhelm Martz 1863 - 1914
(Son of Peter and Alice Martz)

February 16, 1863 - January 5, 1914

Buried at St. Ambrose in Cresaptown,
he is the husband of Annie *Metzner* Martz 1872 - 1935.

Heinrich was the first Martz child born in Cresaptown at the "old Matz place" after Peter and Alice had re-located to Cresaptown following the attack on the 21st Bridge. At some time during his life, he assumed the name of "Henry," the English version of the German "Heinrich," and, with some effort, although the stone is terribly weathered and worn, I am able to read the name of "Henry Martz" on his stone at St. Ambrose.

Indeed, it was both his first and middle names that he chose to anglicize, a fact that I found evident when I researched the *U.S. Census* 1900 thru 1910 and looked at parish records in which Father Thomas in 1914 entered the death and burial not of "Heinrich Wilhelm Martz" but of "Henry William Martz." Notable as well, it seems he was also called by the anglicized "John," as seen on his baptism certificate:

1981 Re-issue of 1863 Certificate

Certificate of Baptism

Ss. Peter & Paul Church
125 FAYETTE STREET
CUMBERLAND, MARYLAND 21502

― This is to Certify ―

That John Henry William Martz
Child of Peter Martz
and Marg. Wigger
born in Cumberland (CITY) Maryland (STATE)
on the 16 day of February 19 1863

was Baptized

on the 26 day of April 19 1863
According to the Rite of the Roman Catholic Church
by the Rev. Wuest
the Sponsors being { Henr. William Tvenner

as appears from the Baptismal Register of this Church.
Dated 7/15/81

Pastor

THE MARTZ CONNECTION

Family Ties:

It is interesting that Heinrich married Annie Metzner, as his sister Margaret married John Metzner, whose newspaper obituary mentions his sister "Mrs. Anna Martz," meaning this Martz brother and sister married a Metzner brother and sister. See John Metzner's obituary when you read about Maggie Metzner in section IX.

Heinrich and Annie lie side-by-side on the gentle slope of St. Ambrose Cemetery in Cresaptown, and their twin stones are each in the form of a Christian cross, two solid crosses standing faithfully together, a sweet tribute to their marriage. Eventually time will erase the names from the stones, so I hope my description of them might one day help another researcher determine who lies beneath the twin crosses.

Heinrich "Henry" Wilhelm Martz
Annie *Metzner* Martz

THE MARTZ CONNECTION

The 1910 *U.S. Census* declares Henry to be a Railroad Trackman and records five children still living in the Winchester Road home of Henry and Annie *Metzner* Martz, who had a total of <u>six</u>, for they had lost their little Anna Josephine in 1902.

Their Six Children:

Edward
Harman
Maria
Francis
Anna Josephine
Elizabeth

Martz Henry	Head	Below is an excerpt from the actual *U. S. Census* of 1910 indicating that Annie gave birth to **6** children but that only **5** were still living. ↓
------ Annie	Wife	
------ Edward	Son	
------ Harman	Son	
------ Maria	Daughter	
------ Francis	Son	
------- Elizabeth	Daughter	
Metzner Edward	Father-in-Law	

↓ ↓

↑
Edward was the father of Annie *Metzner* Martz and was apparently living in this Martz home with his daughter and son-in law in 1910.

The Children of Heinrich Wilhelm Martz:

Edward Henry Martz 1892 - 1976

(Son of Heinrich Wilhelm Martz)

Cumberland Evening Times, October 18, 1976

Edward Henry Martz

"Edward H. Martz, 84, of 1250 Vocke Road, LaVale, died Saturday at Baker VA Center, Martinsburg, where he had been admitted September 14.

A native of Cumberland, he was the son of the late Henry and Annie *Metzner* Martz.

A veteran of WWI, he served with the 57th Corps of Engineers. He was a retired Kelly Springfield Tire Company employee and a member of SS Peter & Paul Catholic Church, Fort Cumberland Post 13 American Legion, United Rubber Workers Local 26, and Allegany County Historical Society.

Surviving are his widow, Florence M. *Gantt* Martz; a daughter, Mrs. Patricia Hout; a son Edward E. Martz; Two sisters, Mrs. Marie Stewart, Mrs. Elizabeth Holt, and two brothers, Harmon and Francis Martz, all of LaVale, and three grandchildren.

Mass of Christian Burial will be celebrated tomorrow at 11 a.m. at SS Peter & Paul Church. Interment will be in Sunset Memorial Park."

CAVEAT:

<u>Another and *Different* Edward Martz</u>:

Edward (Martz) Mallory
The Actor

Edward Ralph Martz 1930 - 2007 was an accomplished actor who adopted the stage name of "Edward Mallory," and he is buried at SS Peter & Paul Cemetery in Cumberland, but he is **not** a descendant of Peter and Alice *Wigger* Martz.

I feel it necessary to issue this caveat because this actor's name understandably comes up when a discussion is raised about the Martz family of Allegany County.

Mr. Mallory (Edward Ralph Martz) played the role of Dr. Bill Horton on the television soap opera " Days of Our Lives," a role he portrayed with distinction for 14 years, propelling him to considerable popularity.

I am not saying Mr. Mallory (Edward Ralph Martz) is not more-distantly related to the Martz subjects of this book. I am, however, declaring that this Hollywood actor is not a descendant of Peter and Alice *Wigger* Martz and therefore is not included in *this* family history except in this caveat. Perhaps he is a descendant of some brother or Cousin of Peter Martz. Even if so, however, that would render him irrelevant to this presentation of the descendants of the Martz family whose home suffered the attack on the 21st Bridge.

Once more, even at the risk of redundancy, please be reminded that this is a history of specifically and solely the progeny of Allegany County's Peter and Alice *Wigger* Martz.

Harman Julius Martz 1894 - 1983

(Son of Heinrich Wilhelm Martz)

September 27, 1894 - May 13, 1983

Harman is Buried at Saint Ambrose Cemetery in Cresaptown.

Cumberland Evening Times
May 15, 1983

"Harman J. Martz, 88, of Winchester Road, died Friday in the Martinsburg VA Center. Born in Allegany County, he was a son of the late Henry Martz and Anna *Metzner* Martz.

Mr. Martz was a retired laborer in the construction industry, was an Army veteran of WWI, a member of Fort Cumberland Post 13 American Legion, and Haystack Mountain Sportsmen's Club.

He is survived by a brother, Francis Joseph Martz, LaVale; two sisters, Mrs. Marie Helen Stewart, LaVale, and Mrs. Elizabeth Catherine Holt, Winchester Road; and a nephew with whom he resided, Richard A. Holt.

A Christian Wake Service will be held in the Hafer Chapel of The Hills Mortuary Monday at 8 p.m.

Friends will be received at the funeral home Sunday 7 to 9 p.m. and Monday 2 to 4 and 7 to 9 p.m.

The Mass of Christian Burial will be celebrated Tuesday at 10 a.m. at Saint Ambrose Catholic Church. Interment will be in the parish cemetery."

On Harman's *Draft Registration Card,* he listed his occupation as "Farming" and stated he was employed by his mother, which makes sense because Harman was 23 and single when he registered in June of 1917, and his father Heinrich had died just three years earlier.

Parish records indicate that Harman was 88 years old and, just like his brother Edward, died at the VA Hospital in Martinsburg.

His Signature on His Draft Card, June 5, 1917

Edward and his brother Harman registered for the draft on the same day, and both of them passed away at the VA Hospital in Martinsburg.

Marie Helen *Martz* Stewart 1896 - 1986

(Daughter of Heinrich Wilhelm Martz)

September 18, 1896 - March 13, 1986
Buried at Saint Ambrose Cemetery in Cresaptown

Cumberland Times News
Saturday, March 15 1986

"Mrs. Marie H. Stewart, 89, formerly of McDonald Road, LaVale, died Thursday at Meyersdale, Pa., Manor Nursing Home.

Born in LaVale September 18, 1896, Mrs. Stewart was the daughter of the late Henry Martz and Annie *Metzner* Martz. Her husband was the late Roy Stewart.

Survivors include one sister, Mrs. Elizabeth Holt, Winchester Road; two nieces and two nephews.

Friends will be received at the Hafer Chapel of the Hills Mortuary Sunday from 2 to 4 and 7 to 9 p.m."

THE MARTZ CONNECTION

Marie *Martz* Stewart

Marie's obituary in 1986 mentions no surviving child. However, her husband Roy's obituary mentions a daughter, Mildred *Stewart* LaPorta, whom we know to have lived until 1998, leaving me to conclude that Mildred was the daughter of Roy but not of Marie:

Roy Stewart
(Husband of Marie *Martz* Stewart)

Cumberland Times News
October 14, 1963

"Roy Stewart, 78, McDonald Road, LaVale, died last night in Memorial Hospital where he was admitted Friday.

He was born in Eckhart, the son of the late John and Mary *Watson* Stewart. He was a member of Welsh Memorial Baptist Church, Frostburg.

He is survived by his widow, Mrs. Marie *Martz* Stewart; one daughter, Mrs. Mildred LaPorta, Eckhart; one grandchild and one great-grandchild.

The body is at the Durst Funeral Home, Frostburg, where friends will be received today from 7 to 9 p.m. and tomorrow from 2 to 4 p.m."

Roy's Previous Marriage:

The evidence, therefore, causes me to believe that Roy was previously married to Minnie *Dudley* Stewart, who died in 1940, and that Mildred *Stewart* LaPorta is a daughter of that previous marriage, for Roy, Minnie, and Mildred are all buried in Eckhart, while Marie *Martz* Stewart is buried among the Martzes of Cresaptown at Saint Ambrose Cemetery.

Francis Joseph Martz 1898 - 1984

(Son of Heinrich Wilhelm Martz)

He was the husband of Helen L. *Spitznas* Martz 1904 - 1999.

Francis and Helen are buried in Frostburg Memorial Park

Frostburg Memorial Park,
70 Green Street, Frostburg, Maryland

THE MARTZ CONNECTION

Cumberland Times-News, February 2, 1984:

"Francis J. Martz, 85, of 540 Henry Drive, LaVale, died Thursday in Lions Manor Nursing Home.

Born in the Winchester Road area, he was a son of the late Henry Martz and Annie *Metzner* Martz. He was retired from the *Cumberland Brewing Company* and was a member of SS Peter & Paul Catholic Church.

He is survived by his widow, Helen *Spitznas* Martz; two sisters, Mrs. Maria Stewart, LaVale, and Mrs. Elizabeth Holt, Winchester Road; and several nieces and nephews.

Friends will be received at Hafer Chapel of the Hill Mortuary Thursday from 7 to 9 p.m. and Friday from 2 to 4 and 7 to 9 p.m."

Francis and Helen's property in the Winchester Bridge section were among the several properties that were taken for the development of the Country Club Mall in LaVale, and a newspaper article that reports on the intention to take the properties also shows that other descendents of Peter and Alice Martz were impacted by the government's ability to seize private property in the name of civic improvement.

Specifically, the imposed-upon Martzes named in the article, those who would eventually lose their homes and experience the conclusive authority of "eminent domain" were thus:

<u>Mary *Martz* Athey</u>, <u>Ursula *Martz* Kuhlman</u>,
<u>Francis Martz</u>, and <u>Helen Martz</u>

Mary *Martz* Athey and Ursula *Martz* Kuhlman are daughters of Martin Joseph Martz, and, of course, Francis is a son of Heinrich Martz, so the article rather demonstrates the close proximity in which these Martzes lived. Moreover, their being both family and neighbors must have made it especially heart-wrenching to have to give up their homes:

The Cumberland News, December 30, 1971:

Rezoning Hearing Set in LaVale
SHOPPING MALL IS PROPOSED

"A public hearing has been scheduled by the LaVale Zoning Board for 7:45 p.m. Tuesday, January 11 at the LaVale Fire Hall on a proposal to change the zoning of an 84 acre tract near the intersection of Winchester and Vocke Roads.

The application calls for an amendment to the zoning map of the LaVale Zoning District to change the classification of the 84 acres from Residential A and Rural Residential to Commercial A.

It is understood that a developer is interested in building a shopping mall in an oval shaped area extending on the easterly side of Winchester Road to Grabenstein Road.

Rather than engage in extensive excavations, it is understood that the tentative plans call for the development of the shopping mall at an elevation almost 100 feet higher than the present level of Vocke Road.

The property is adjacent to the Cover Valley Golf Course but does not include the course.

Owners of the property on which the application has been filed for rezoning are John A. Border, Doris L. Border, Harold Barmoy, Mary A. Barmoy, **Mary *Martz* Athey**, **Ursula *Martz* Kuhlman**, Samuel W. Border, Maria M. Border, William C. Hartman, Florence Hartman, Orain L. Twigg, Alberta M. Twigg, **Francis Martz**, **Helen Martz**, Clarence C. Myers, Vienna J. Myers, and Cover Valley Corporation..."

Change in the name of progress is inevitable. Still, after researching these Martzes, I cannot find myself in the Country Club Mall or its parking lot without feeling a measure of resentment for "eminent domain," but also a bit of nostalgia for a simpler, more-predictable yesterday.

Anna Josephine Martz 1902 - 1902
(Daughter of Heinrich Wilhelm Martz)

Born October 11, 1902 Died November 16, 1902
Age 36 Days

In St. Ambrose Cemetery, at the foot of the graves of Henry and Annie, this stone is barely legible and was at first a great mystery to this writer, who, without definitive proof feels all but certain that this is a child of Henry and Annie.

Legible German Inscription:

> ANNA JOSEPHINE
> MARTZ
> *Geb. den 11 Oct 1902*
> *Gest. den 16*
> *Nov 1902*

English Translation:

> ANNA JOSEPHINE
> MARTZ
> Born the 11th of Oct 1902
> Died the 16th
> of Nov 1902

THE MARTZ CONNECTION

My purpose in thus transcribing this information from Anna Josephine's stone is that time is having its way, and I want to secure Anna in at least this book, as the record of her life becomes more and more obscure, especially that record that was once so clearly established in stone.

I came across Anna's stone at St. Ambrose Cemetery, noting that it lay at the foot of Henry's and Annie's burial plot, between Annie's mother, Johanna Metzner, and Annie's son, Harman. She had been only a baby, living only a month, but I had no way of determining the relationships. I did not know, that is, just whose child this was.

When I discovered it, the time-worn, weather-worn marker was lying flat on the ground, having become detached from the embedded base-stone that had once anchored it to the earth. It was becoming illegible, and its being not secured to the earth means it could easily be carried off or displaced, all of which made me very sad to realize that no one seemed to care anymore about this little stone whose purpose was to memorialize a child who was certainly loved by *someone*—by some of these Martzes and Metzners, in fact. The sight of this neglected little stone stirred in me an emotion not unlike the way one might feel when discovering a neglected child, and I instantly felt a responsibility to at least *try* to preserve her identity.

Researching in the 1910 *U.S. Census*, I discovered the data entered that year for Annie *Metzner* Martz indicating that she had given birth to 6 children but that only 5 of them were still living, thereby declaring she did in fact have a child who had died.

Therefore, unable to find any documentation that would suggest otherwise, and especially given that Anna Josephine lies at the feet of Henry and Annie, whom we know to have lost a child, I have included her as indeed their child, intent with all sincerity to not lose *anyone* through the sieve of history.

Anna Josephine Martz, age 36 days,
lies at rest beside her brother Harman
at the foot of her parents, Henry and Annie:

At the bottom of Anna Josephine's Stone:

"Bis auf Wiedersehen"
"Until we meet again"

Elizabeth Catherine *Martz* Holt 1907 - 2007

(Daughter of Heinrich Wilhelm Martz)

Buried at SS Peter & Paul Cemetery,
she lived to be 100 years old.

Cumberland Times-News, March 27, 2007:

"Elizabeth Catherine Holt, 100, of LaVale, died Saturday, March 24, 2007, at The Beverly Living Center.

Born January 1, 1907 in LaVale, she was the daughter of the late Henry and Annie *Metzner* Martz.

She was also preceded in death by her husband, Adrian Marion Holt; her daughter, Hilda Gellner; her sister, Marie H. Stewart; and three brothers, Edward H. Martz, Harman Martz, and Francis J. Martz.

Mrs. Martz was a member of SS Peter & Paul Catholic Church, Cresaptown Senior Citizens, and Red-Cross Warm up Across America program. She loved to crochet and made blankets for nursing home residents.

Survivors include her son, Richard A. Holt, and wife Naomi, of LaVale; five grandchildren, Janet Jones, and husband Chris, John Holt, and wife Renae, Darlene Cosner, and husband, Tim, Mike Gellner, and wife Sandy, and Jeffry Gellner, and wife Karen; 11 great grandchildren; and several step-great grandchildren."

V

JOHANNES BERNHART

"BERNARD"

Johannes Bernhart Martz 1865 - 1941
(Son of Peter and Alice Martz)

October 10, 1865 - July 6, 1941

From his obituary, his sons' obituaries,
the *U.S. Census*, and parish records:

Buried at SS Peter & Paul Cemetery in Cumberland,
he is the husband of Mary Teresa *Neis* Martz 1860 - 1929
with whom he had the following two sons:

William Bernard Martz
August 11, 1892 - January 21, 1941
(Buried in SS Peter & Paul Cemetery)

Ralph Andrew Martz
January 10, 1897 - February 28, 1926
(Buried in SS Peter & Paul Cemetery)

1981 Reissue of 1865 Certificate

Certificate of Baptism

Ss. Peter & Paul Church
125 FAYETTE STREET
CUMBERLAND, MARYLAND 21502

This is to Certify

That John Bernard Martz

Child of Peter Martz

and Marg. Adelh. Wiggert

born in Allegany County (CITY) _____ (STATE)

on the 7 (10) day of October 1865

was **Baptized**

on the 31 day of December 1865

According to the Rite of the Roman Catholic Church by the Rev. Frischbier

the Sponsors being { John Bern. Wiggert / Maria Cath. Schulte }

as appears from the Baptismal Register of this Church.

Dated 7/15/81

Pastor

As do many children of immigrants, Johannes Bernhart Martz took on an anglicized version of his given name, which is why his gravestone bears the name "Bernard J. Martz."

Johannes Bernhart Martz

Johannes Bernhart, or "Bernard," who had been born at the "old 'Matz' place" in Cresaptown, worked at the *Cumberland Brewing Company* for 45 years. His son William died in January of 1941, and at about that same time Johannes' ill-health forced him to retire from the brewery, and he died just six months later in July of 1941 at age 75.

A 1917 Cumberland City Directory shows he was a foreman at the brewery and that he lived at 338 N. Mechanic Street, which would have given him an easy walk to work.

But Johannes, pictured at left, would not be the only brewer in the family, for his sister Anna's son John Julius Boch (1884 - 1962) would also retire from the *Cumberland Brewing Company,* and his brother Heinrich's son Francis J. Martz (1898 - 1984) also later retired from the same brewery.

The *Cumberland Brewing Company* (1890 - 1958), which operated on North Centre Street, produced Old Export Beer and Gamecock Ale. It was the oldest major brewing company that operated in Cumberland. It was purchased by *Queen City Brewing Company* in 1958 and was the last surviving brewery in Cumberland when it closed its doors in 1976.

Johannes was a member of the *Holy Name Society* and was a knight of the *Catholic Knights of America.*

Pallbearers for Johannes "Bernard" Martz were: Francis J. Martz, John J. Boch, William R. Taylor, H. B. Harden, Herman J. Grabenstein, and Charles F. Strong.

According to the *Cumberland Evening Times* Obituary of July 7, 1941, Johannes Bernhart Martz died "at the home of his daughter-in-law, Mrs. Margaret M. Martz," at 520 North Mechanic Street in Cumberland. It was the home of his daughter-in-law because his son William had died less than six months earlier. It seems therefore that the aging Johannes had lived with his son and daughter-in-law until his son died, and that he continued to live with his daughter-in-law for another six months until his own death.

The Children of Johannes Bernhart Martz:

William Bernard Martz 1891 - 1941
(Son of Johannes Bernhart Martz)

William was the husband of <u>Margaret *Uhl* Martz</u>.

Born August 11, 1891, William was 25 years old when he registered for the WWI Draft on June 5, 1917. His Draft Card tells us he was of medium height and build and had brown hair and blue eyes. Upon his registration, he reported having two dependents: a wife and one child. At that time, William, lived at 338 North Mechanic Street with his wife and that only child.

His signature on his Draft Card, June 5, 1917

The Household of William B. Martz
In the 1930 *U.S. Census:*

William, 38, Head
Margaret, 34, Wife
William, 13, Son
Evelyn, 9, Daughter
Helen, 5, Daughter

William is buried at SS Peter & Paul Cemetery.

Cumberland Evening Times, January 22, 1941:

"William B. Martz, 49, of 520 North Mechanic street, money order clerk at the Cumberland Post Office, died this morning. He had been at the Post Office since 1910. He is survived by his wife, Mrs. Margaret M. *Uhl* Martz; his father, Bernard J. Martz; one son, William B. Martz; and two daughters, Mrs. John Wolfhope and Miss Helen Martz. He was a member of Cumberland Council #586 Knights of Columbus, The Holy Name Society of SS Peter & Paul Church, and of the Federation of Post Office Employees.

Mr. Martz, though troubled with a heart ailment for a long time, was seriously ill for only three days."

Ralph Andrew Martz 1897 - 1926
(Son of Johannes Bernhart Martz)

Husband of Mary *Struntz* (Martz) Knieriem,

Ralph and Mary had one child, who was Ralph Andrew Martz, Jr., whose name was changed to
Ralph Andrew Knieriem

Ralph's headstone in SS Peter & Paul Cemetery indicates he was born in 1897, but on his Draft Card he states he was born January 10, 1896. Without inordinate pondering on this discrepancy, I entered (above) his birth year as 1897 because, in this book, I always go with the dates that are literally written in stone, accepting the inevitable uncertainties that we uncover when researching history. Moreover, his newspaper obituary indicates he was 29 when he died in March of 1926, so the math has him born in 1897, disputing the card and confirming the stone.

Ralph reported on his Draft Card that he was employed by "United Accessories Company," which was an automobile accessory company that had a store in Cumberland that started in business April 1, 1915 at 20 North Center Street before expanding and moving to the corner of Frederick St.

His Signature on His Draft Card, June 5, 1918

Cumberland Evening Times
March 1, 1926

Ralph Andrew Martz

"Ralph A. Martz, 29 years old, a salesman, died of Scarlet Fever at his home, 632 North Mechanic Street, yesterday.

The funeral, which was private, was held at 4 o'clock this afternoon. Father Simon, of SS Peter & Paul Catholic Church, officiated. Burial was in SS Peter & Paul Cemetery.

Mr. Martz is survived by his parents, Mr. and Mrs. Bernard Martz; his wife, Mrs. Mary *Struntz* Martz, and a son, Ralph A. Martz Jr., two years old.

Mr. Martz contracted influenza while in the Army during the World War and is said never to have since been healthy."

At the time of this publication, there is still no vaccine to prevent Scarlet Fever. Anyone can contract the disease, but it was a leading cause of death of children in the early 1900's.

THE MARTZ CONNECTION

RALPH ANDREW MARTZ
WAS MARRIED TO :

Mary Madeline *Struntz* (Martz) Knieriem

Cumberland Sunday Times, September 12, 1982

MRS. GUSTAVE KNIERIEM

"Mrs. Mary Madeline Knieriem, of 502 Franklin Street, died Friday at her residence.

Born in Wrights Crossing, Frostburg, she was the daughter of the late Antone Struntz and Marie *Panzer* Struntz. She also was proceeded in death by two husbands, Ralph A. Martz and Gustave Knieriem.

Mrs. Knieriem was a former thoroughbred race horse owner and trainer and enjoyed prominence in the field of thoroughbred horses. Among her best-known horses were Red Wrack, king of the half-milers; and Lena Girl and Aylesbury. She retired from training and racing in the early 1960's.

She also was a member of SS Peter & Paul Catholic Church and the Third Order of Saint Francis.

Surviving are a brother, Alec R. Struntz, Annan Knolls, Cresaptown; three grandchildren, Mary Ethel Patterson, Bethel Park, Pa.; Ralph A. Knieriem Jr., Manassas, Va; Gustave A. Knieriem, Washington, DC., and four great-grandchildren.

Mass of the Christian Burial will be celebrated Monday, 9:30 a.m. at SS Peter & Paul. Interment will be in the parish cemetery.

Pallbearers will be John Billard, Thomas Struntz, James Struntz, Joseph Struntz, and Doug Brown. Honorary pallbearers will be William C. Knieriem, James Lyons, and Henry D. Stevens."

Note:

Ralph Andrew Martz died in 1926 at the age of 29, leaving his widow Mary with a 2-year-old son, Ralph Andrew Martz, Jr.. Subsequently, when Mary remarried, her new husband adopted her son, which explains why Peter and Alice Wigger Martz have a great-grandson named "Ralph Andrew Knieriem."

VI

MARTIN JOSEPH

Martin Joseph Martz 1869 - 1946
(Son of Peter and Alice Martz)

Buried in SS Peter & Paul Cemetery in Cumberland, he is the husband of <u>Elizabeth M. *Marley* Martz 1883 - 1954</u>.

1981 Reissue of 1868 Certificate

Certificate of Baptism

Ss. Peter & Paul Church
125 FAYETTE STREET
CUMBERLAND, MARYLAND 21502

This is to Certify

That Martin Joseph (Marz) Martz
Child of Peter Martz
and Adelheid Wigger
born in Baltimore (CITY) Maryland (STATE)
on the 27 (24) day of June 1868
was **Baptized**
on the 9 day of August 1868
According to the Rite of the Roman Catholic Church
by the Rev. Cyril Knoll
the Sponsors being Martin Wigger

as appears from the Baptismal Register of this Church.

Dated 7/15/81

Rev. Rot Charles
9b   Pastor

The years of Martin Joseph (1869 - 1946) and the years of Elizabeth (1883 - 1954) are correct on their gravestones, notwithstanding the faulty records I have discovered on the internet. As we have precious little information on Martin Joseph, we should at least get correct this very basic information, which can be easily verified by simply going to the gravestones and reading.

His Wife

Cumberland Evening Times, September 20, 1940:

"A birthday surprise party was given Tuesday night for Mrs. Martin Martz, Allegany Grove [Allegany Grove is in the LaVale area]. Cards and refreshments featured. Those present were Misses Margaret Metzner, Lucy Martz, Mary Catherine Metzner, Marie Sittig, Fred Martz, Mr. and Mrs. Clarence Martz, Mr. and Mrs. Wm. Kuhlman and family, Mr. and Mrs. James Martz, Mr. and Mrs. Jack Pasial and daughter, Theresa, Mr. and Mrs. George Martz, Mr. and Mrs. Adrian Holt and daughter Hilda, Mr. and Mrs. Martin Martz, Mr. and Mrs. Raymond Spies, Mr. and Mrs. Ralph Athey and family, Mr. and Mrs. Robert Broadwater, Mrs. S. K. Crist, and Edward Grabenstein."

The preceding article mentions "Allegany Grove," which is in LaVale. Also, the *U.S. Census* of 1920, 1930, and 1940 all list Martin Joseph Martz as an employee of the railroad (as a trackman in 1920 and 1930 and as a railroad repairman in 1940), citing his residence as LaVale, and J. Marshall Porter mentions at least one of Martin's children attending the Winchester Bridge School, which was located near the LaVale end of Winchester Road.

His Children

From the *U.S. Census* records, obituaries, parish records, and from J. Marshall Porter's memory as preserved in *Hallowed Be This Land,* I proffer the following list of twelve children born to Martin Joseph Martz and Elizabeth *Marley* Martz:

Joseph 1893 - 1910
Frederick 1895 - 1980
George 1896 - 1966
Lucille 1897 - 1974
Charles 1899 - 1974
Clara 1902 - 1961
Clarence 1903 - 1951
James 1905 - 1953
Mary 1908 - 1979
Lawrence 1909 - 1923
Ursula 1911 - 2001
John 1913 - 1913

THE MARTZ CONNECTION

Cumberland News, April 30, 1946:

MARTIN MARTZ RITES

"Funeral services for Martin Martz, 77, retired Cumberland and Pennsylvania railroad worker, who died early yesterday morning at his home on Route 5, will be conducted tomorrow morning at 10 o'clock in SS Peter & Paul Catholic Church. Interment will be in the church cemetery.

Born near Cresaptown, he was a son of the late Peter and Alice *Wigger* Martz.

He was a member of SS Peter & Paul Catholic Church and the Holy Name Society of the parish.

Besides his widow, Mrs. Elizabeth *Marley* Martz, he is survived by the following children: Frederick, Lucy, and Charles Martz, all at home; George Martz, Roberts Place; Clarence and James Martz, Route 5; Mrs. Garland Poisal, Allegany Grove; Mrs. Ralph Athey, Roberts Place; and Mrs. William Kuhlman, Route 5.

One brother, Peter Martz, Cresaptown; three sisters, Mrs. Mary Metzner, Route 5, Mrs. Catherine Duffner, Syracuse, N.Y., and Mrs. Frances McBee, Westernport, and six grandchildren also survive."

The 1920 *U.S. Census* tells us Martin worked for the *Cumberland & Pennsylvania Railroad* (C&P), which operated in Western Maryland primarily as a coal hauler. It was owned by the *Consolidation Coal Company* and was purchased by the Western Maryland Railway in 1944.

The line ran from Cumberland to Piedmont, at both points interchanging with the B&O Railroad. The C&P shops were located at Mount Savage, also the location of its headquarters. On the way to Piedmont the line passed through (and under) Frostburg, where, at the time of this publication, the C&P station serves as the western terminus of the Western Maryland Scenic Railroad.

The Children of Martin Joseph Martz

Joseph Francis Martz 1893 - 1910

(Son of Martin Joseph Martz)

In his book *Hallowed Be This Land,* on page 78, J. Marshall Porter mentions the death in 1910 of an older classmate at Winchester Bridge School, "Joe Martz," whom Mr. Porter tells us was "around 16" and was a son of "Martin Martz.":

"There were families then who would nearly all come down with Typhoid Fever in late summers, but it was usually traced to the supply of drinking water or some dairy foods, and always took place before school started. Also, not so many children ever got it in proportion to adults. But the fall of 1910, Joe Martz, aged around 16, a fat jolly boy of the Martin Martz family, who, along with most of the members of the family, contracted Typhoid Fever and died from it. His death was a saddening event to all the students because he was kind and helpful to the big and little boys and girls alike. I thought of Joe as a big buddy. The winter before he died, our teacher sent me along with Joe to cut a Christmas tree for the school."

—J. Marshall Porter

The Cumberland Alleganian
Wednesday, November 23, 1910

Victim of Typhoid

"Joseph Martz died Monday at the home of his parents, Martin and Lizzie Martz, on the mountain, back of Allegany Grove, from Typhoid Fever, aged 17 years."

Winchester Bridge School

"Winchester Bridge School," a one-room school heated by a cast-iron potbelly stove, was located at the LaVale end of Winchester Road, where Winchester Road intersected with Vocke Road. That section known as "Winchester Bridge" was named in association with a huge railroad bridge that stood there until it was removed in 1936 in order to widen the road.

The Winchester Bridge School

Both, Marshall Porter and Joseph Martz, and indeed many of the subjects of this book, lived within walking distance of this school, although in those days "walking distance" was a bit farther than it is today.

Adding poignancy to Joe's death is an article about his brother Frederick's birthday party in January of 1912, just fourteen months after Joe's death, a party from which Joe is conspicuously absent, as you will read on the following page.

Frederick Martin Martz 1895 - 1980

(Son of Martin Joseph Martz)

The Evening Times, January 18, 1912:

Surprise Party Above Town

"A surprise party was given in honor of Mr. Frederick Martz's 17th birthday. Those that were present were: Mr. and Mrs. Charles Threscher, Mr. and Mrs. Edward Grabenstein, Mr. and Mrs. Martin Martz, Mr. Jerome Burkey, Mr. Frank Vocke, Mrs. Margaret Metzner, Peter Grabenstein, George Boch, Frederick Martz, Leonard McKenzie, Troubadour Lewis, Marshall Porter, Joseph Metzner, Lawrence Martz, Elizabeth Grabenstein, Frances Burkey, Dora Lewis, Rosa Threscher, Clara Grabenstein, Bertie Porter, Lucy Martz, Frances Boch, Anna Burkey, Mary Margaret Vocke, Clara Martz, and Ursula Martz. Refreshments were served at a late hour."

From the 1920 *U.S. Census,* I discovered that Frederick became a fireman for the Western Maryland Railroad.

The railroad "fireman" managed the output of steam. His boiler had to respond to frequent changes in demand for power. A skilled fireman anticipated changing demand as he fed coal to the firebox and water to the boiler. At the same time, the fireman was the "copilot" of the train who knew the signals, curves, and grade changes as well as the engineer.

Notwithstanding his job with the Railroad in his younger years, however, Frederick must have eventually settled into a life of farming, for he was a retired farmer when he died in 1980:

The Death of Frederick Martin Martz

Cumberland Evening Times
February 27, 1980

"Frederick M. Martz, 85, Martz Lane Extended, LaVale, died yesterday in Dennett Road Manor Nursing Home, Oakland.

Born on Winchester Road, LaVale, he was the son of the late Martin Martz and Mary Elizabeth *Marley* Martz.

He was a retired farmer, a member of SS Peter & Paul Church and was an honorary member of the Haystack Sportsmen Club.

Surviving are one sister, Mrs. Ursula L. Kuhlman, LaVale, and a number of nieces and nephews.

Friends will be received from 7 to 9 p.m. today and 2 to 4 and 7 to 9 p.m. tomorrow at the George Funeral Home.

Mass of the Christian Burial will be conducted Friday at 10 a.m. in the SS Peter & Paul Church.

Interment will be in the parish cemetery.

A wake service will be conducted at 8 p.m. tomorrow in the funeral home."

The Draft Card Mystery of Frederick Martin Martz

The two preceding newspaper articles, one about a surprise party and the other his obituary, mutually confirm his birth year as <u>1895</u>. Moreover, his headstone is marked as <u>1895</u>. However, as you see on the following page, his Draft Card claims his birth year as <u>1894</u>:

[Registration Card for Frederick M. Martz, showing age 22, residence La Vale, Cumberland, Md., date of birth January 16, 1894, Natural Born citizen, born Winchester, City?, Maryland, U.S.A., occupation Farmer, employed by Father at La Vale, single, White, signed Frederick M. Martz]

Here we can be grateful for the legible handwriting of a Draft Registrar, and by comparing his handwriting with Frederick's, we see it was he, and not Frederick, who filled out the card.

We can imagine the registrar entering the information as he interviews Frederick, but the mystery is to how that interview ended with the presumably-incorrect birth year.

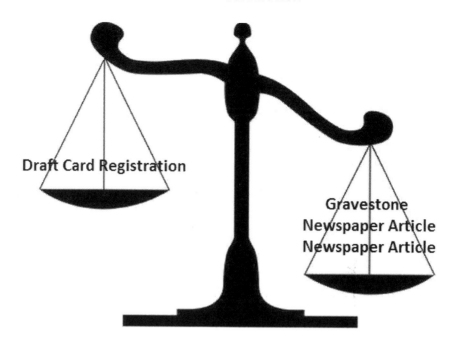

In a court of law, the case is not decided by the number of witnesses on either side. It is, however, decided by credibility and corroboration, and, in this case in particular, I consider the gravestone and the newspaper articles to be both corroborating and credible, which is why this book enters into record the birth year of Frederick Martin Martz as 1895.

Aside from technicality, however, did you notice how Frederick answered question 5 on the card?

5 Where were you born?: "Winchester Bridge, Maryland U.S.A."

That should lay to rest any doubt that Winchester Bridge was not only a bridge but also a geographical location, a *neighborhood.*

Finally, on the back of this card was entered a physical description of Frederick Martin Martz, who is described as being tall and slender, with black hair and brown eyes.

George Andrew Martz 1896 - 1966

(Son of Martin Joseph Martz)

March 29, 1896 - January 23, 1966

Cumberland Evening Times, January 24, 1966:

"George Andrew Martz, 69, of 21 National Highway, was dead on arrival yesterday at Sacred Heart Hospital.

A native of Winchester Road, Cumberland, he was a son of the late Martin and Mary Elizabeth *Marley* Martz.

Mr. Martz retired several years ago as an employee of Street's Body Works. He was a veteran of World War I and a member of Henry Hart Post 1411 VFW and SS Peter & Paul Catholic Church. He also was a trustee of Haystack Sportsman's Club.

Surviving are his wife, Margaret R. *Stonebraker* Martz; two brothers, Fred and Charles Martz, Winchester Bridge; and three sisters, Miss Lucy Martz and Mrs. William Kuhlman, Winchester Bridge; and Mrs. Ralph Athey, Robert's Place.

Requiem Mass will be celebrated Wednesday at 9 a.m. at SS Peter & Paul Church, and burial will be in the parish cemetery."

His Signature On His Draft Card, June 5, 1917

According to a description on the back of his draft card, George was of medium height and build, with black hair and brown eyes.

George Andrew Martz
With His Wife, a Sister, and Two Brothers

George, Margaret, Frederick, Lucy, and Charles

This Martz plot is rather obviously marked with the above-pictured stone. The flat stone at left is marked as "George A. Martz," and that on the right is marked as "Margaret R. Martz," his wife.

On the ground at the back side of this stone are the flat markers of George's brothers Frederick and Charles, and his sister Lucy.

This plot is in SS Peter & Paul Cemetery and is located not far off of Fayette Street. One with very good eyesight might read the name of Martz from the street.

Lucille Cecelia Martz 1897 - 1974

(Daughter of Martin Joseph Martz)

"Lucy"

November 12, 1897 - December 27, 1974

Note the above declaration that Lucy's life came to an end in 1974, because there is conflicting information regarding the year of her death. The *Social Security Death Index,* that is, incorrectly claims she died in Sykesville, Maryland "January 15, 1975," but a visit to her grave at SS Peter & Paul Cemetery in Cumberland will afford you the opportunity to see her headstone that clearly encapsulates her lifespan:

I think many of us like to believe we can trust our government to keep accurate records, but in this case, when I have to choose between government records [1975] and that which is literally written in stone [1974], I will believe the stone.

Note also that her headstone proclaims "SISTER" and not "MOTHER" or "WIFE." That's because Lucy apparently remained single all her life, a fact supported by each *U.S. Census* from 1900 to 1940, for at each census she is listed as single and living in her parents' house. Furthermore, her obituary in the *Cumberland Evening Times* mentioned no husband or children, all of which is evidence of her having remained single.

In the 1920 census, at the age of 22, Lucy's occupation is listed as "Presser" in the industry of "Dye Works."

Two decades forward, in the 1940 census, she is listed as a "Nurse" in the industry of "Pvt Nurse" and the "Class of Worker" is listed as "Working on Own Account." Given that her father was at that time nearing the end of his life, I have to wonder whether her nursing was either wholly or in part a service rendered to the man in whose home she was living.

Her sister Clara's obituary in 1961 states that Lucy and her brother Charles are both living in Sykesville, Maryland in 1961, and Sykesville would be her last residence according to the *Social Security Death Index.*

In her brother George's obituary in 1966 (See George Andrew Martz), we see listed a sister "Miss Lucy Martz," the "Miss" being further evidence of her remaining single throughout her life.

Cumberland Evening Times, December 28, 1974:

"Miss Lucy Martz, 77, of Martz Lane, LaVale, died yesterday at Memorial Hospital. Born in LaVale, Miss Martz was a daughter of the late Martin and Elizabeth *Marley* Martz.
Miss Martz was a registered nurse and a graduate of Allegany School of Nursing. She was a member of St. Patrick's Catholic Church and the Catholic Daughters of America.
Surviving are two sisters, Mrs. Mary M. Athey, Bowling Green and Mrs. Ursula L. Kuhlman, LaVale, and a brother, Frederick Martz, LaVale.

The body is at the George Funeral Home where friends will be received today from 7 to 9 p.m. and tomorrow from 2 to 4 and 7 to 9 p.m.

Mass of the Christian Burial will be celebrated Monday at 11 a.m. at St. Patrick's Church. Burial will be in SS Peter & Paul Cemetery.

The CDA will recite the rosary tomorrow at 8 p.m. at the funeral home."

Allegany Hospital on Decatur Street in Cumberland

Lucy Martz was a graduate of the Allegany Hospital School of Nursing.

Built in 1905 and turned over to the direction of the Catholic Daughters of Charity in 1911, the name was changed from Allegany Hospital to Sacred Heart Hospital in 1952, and it was moved to Seton Drive on Haystack Mountain in 1967.

Charles Edward Martz 1899 - 1974

(Son of Martin Joseph Martz)

Cumberland Evening Times, June 27, 1974:

"Charles E. Martz, 74, of Martz Lane, LaVale died yesterday after a lingering illness.

Born in LaVale, he was a son of the late Martin and Elizabeth *Marley* Martz.

A retired barber, he was a member of SS Peter & Paul Catholic Church.

Surviving are three sisters, Miss Lucy C. Martz, city, Mrs. Mary M. Athey, Bowling Green, and Mrs. Ursula L. Kuhlman, LaVale, and a brother, Frederick M. Martz, LaVale.

The body is at the George Funeral Home where friends will be received from 7 until 9 p.m. today and from 2 until 4 and 7 until 9 p.m. tomorrow.

Mass of Christian Burial will be celebrated Saturday at 10 a.m. at SS Peter & Paul Catholic Church. Burial will be in the parish cemetery.

A Christian wake service will be held at the funeral home tomorrow at 8 p.m."

Charles and Sister Lucy in Sykesville:

When we read his sister Clara's obituary (See Clara C. *Martz* Poisal), we see Charles and sister Lucy both lived in Sykesville in 1961, and the *Social Security Death Index* declares his last residence to have been in Sykesville.

Each consecutive census describes him as being single, which makes it interesting to me that Charles and his sister Lucille, who also remained single, both ended up living in Sykesville, and I am curious as to how they might have migrated to that part of the state.

Finally, however, I would not be much of a romantic if I failed to notice that both Lucy and Charles died in 1974, for Lucy died just six months after the death of her brother, and both returned to Cumberland and are buried in SS Peter & Paul Cemetery.

FADLEY

**Lucy and Charles
Sister and Brother**

Both lived in Sykesville,
both died in 1974, and they are buried side by side
at SS Peter & Paul.

Clara Catherine *Martz* Poisal 1902 - 1961
(Daughter of Martin Joseph Martz)

Cumberland Evening Times, July 10, 1961:

Poisal, Mrs. Clara Catherine *Martz*

"W.Va.—Mrs. Charles G. Poisal—Mrs. Clara Catherine Poisal, 59, of Camp Ground Road, LaVale, died Saturday night in Sacred Heart Hospital where she had been admitted earlier in the day. Born in the Winchester Road section, she was the daughter of the late Martin and Elizabeth *Marley* Martz. Mrs. Poisal was a member of SS Peter & Paul Catholic Church and the Christian Mothers. Surviving, besides her husband, are a daughter, Mrs. Carl W. Leasure, LaVale; three brothers, George and Fred Martz, both of LaVale, and Charles Martz, Sykesville; three sisters, Miss Lucille Martz, Sykesville, Mrs. Robert Athey, Roberts Place, and Mrs. William Kuhlman, LaVale, and a grandson. The body is at the John J. Hafer Chapel of The Hills Mortuary, U.S. 40 and Braddock Road, where the family will receive friends from 2 to 4 p.m.

A Requiem Mass will be celebrated Wednesday at 9 a.m. at SS Peter & Paul Church. Burial will be in the parish cemetery. The Rosary will be recited tomorrow at 8 p.m."

RIP

Throughout this book, the reader encounters the Latin phrase "Requiem Mass," which is a Mass for the dead. The best known part of this Mass is the phrase "Requiescat aeternam dona eis, Domine," which means "Grant them eternal rest, O Lord."

"Requiescat in Pace" is a Latin phrase or prayer that, when simplified for English speakers, means "Rest in Peace," a prayer and sentiment we often see abbreviated on headstones as "R.I.P."

Clarence Julius Martz 1903 - 1951

(Son of Martin Joseph Martz)

In the 1920 *U.S. Census* Clarence was 16 years old in his father's house and was a "Helper" on the farm.

From the 1930 *U.S. Census,* I learned that Clarence, age 26, was a "tire repairer" in a "tire plant," so we might presume "tire plant" to have been the recently opened Kelly Springfield Company in Cumberland.

The 1940 *U.S. Census* shows that Clarence was 35 and was then an "Acetate Worker," which suggests he was likely working at the Celanese Corporation, the world's largest producer of vinyl acetate monomer.

Cumberland Evening Times, September 20, 1951:

"Clarence Julius Martz, 48, of Route 5 of this city died this morning in Allegany Hospital where he had been a patient the past 10 days.
An employee of the Cellulose Acetate Department of the Amcelle Plant of Celanese Corporation, he had been in failing health the past year.
He was a member of SS Peter & Paul Catholic Church and the Haystack Rod and Gun Club.
Mr. Martz was born at Route 5, this city, and was the son of Elizabeth *Marley* Martz and the late Martin Martz.
Besides his mother, he is survived by his wife, Mrs. Zora *Hendrickson* Martz; four brothers, Fredrick Martz and Charles Martz, at home, James Martz of Route 5, and George Martz of Narrows Park, and four sisters, Miss Lucille Martz, at home; Mrs. Garland Poisal, Allegany Grove; Mrs. Ralph Athey, Roberts Place, and Mrs. William Kuhlman of Route 5.
...Interment will be in the Church Cemetery."

James Bernard Martz 1905 - 1953

(Son of Martin Joseph Martz)

Cumberland Evening Times, January 29, 1953:

James B. Martz

"James Bernard Martz, 47, Vocke Drive, died this morning in Memorial Hospital where he had been a patient since January 9. He had been in failing health since 1947.

He was born August 9, 1905 on Vocke Drive, the son of Mrs. Elizabeth *Marley* Martz and the late Martin Martz.

Until 1947, Mr. Martz had been employed by the Cumberland Brewing Company.

Besides his mother who lives on Vocke Drive, he is survived by his wife, Mrs. Lillian *Shirey* Martz ; three brothers, George Martz, Narrows Park, and Fred Martz and Charles Martz, both of RD 5; and four sisters, Miss Lucy Martz, and Mrs. William Kuhlman, both of RD 5, Mrs. Garland Poisal, Allegany Grove, and Mrs. Ralph Athey, Roberts Place.

He was a member of SS Peter & Paul.

The body is at the residence."

Cumberland Evening Times, February 3, 1953:

Martz Rites

"A Requiem Mass for James B. Martz, 47, Vocke Drive, who died Thursday in Memorial Hospital, was conducted yesterday at SS Peter & Paul Church with Rev. Louis Glantz as celebrant. Burial was in the parish cemetery.

Pallbearers were Francis Martz, Clarence McBee, Harman Martz, Julius Martz, Edward Martz, and Edward Ellsworth."

FADLEY

Mary Margaret *Martz* Athey 1908 - 1979

(Daughter of Martin Joseph Martz)

March 10, 1908 - March 22, 1979

The wife of <u>Ralph Webster Athey</u>

The 1920 *U.S. Census* reports that Martin Joseph Martz and his wife Elizabeth had a 12-year-old daughter named Mary Margaret living with them in the family home at the time of the census.

Cumberland Evening Times, March 23, 1979:

"Mrs. Mary M. Athey, 71, of 12101 Mercury Street, Bowling Green died yesterday in Sacred Heart Hospital.

Born in Cumberland she was a daughter of the late Martin Martz and Elizabeth *Marley* Martz.

She was a member of SS Peter & Paul Catholic Church, the Christian Mothers, and Senior Citizens of Allegany County.

Surviving are her husband Ralph W. Athey; four daughters, Mrs. Mary Ann Vanderhout, Union Grove, Mrs. Joyce E. Wagner, Bethesda, Mrs. Jane C. Bearinger, Bowling Green, Mrs. Susan Rounds, Sterling Park, Virginia; two sons, Robert R. Athey, and Donald J. Athey, both of Bowling Green; a brother, Frederick M. Martz, LaVale, and a sister, Mrs. Ursula L. Coleman, LaVale.

Friends will be received at the George Funeral Home today from 7 to 9 p.m. and tomorrow and from 2 to 4 and 7 to 9 p.m."

Lawrence Aloysius Martz 1909 - 1923

(Son of Martin Joseph Martz)

Cumberland Evening Times, September 10, 1923:

Lawrence Martz

"Lawrence Martz, 14 years of age, son of Mr. and Mrs. Martin Martz, died at the home of his parents near Winchester Bridge yesterday morning. Besides his parents, he is survived by the following brothers and sisters: Frederick, George, Charles, Clarence, James, Lucille, Clara, Mary, and Ursula.

The funeral will be held tomorrow morning at 10 o'clock with services at SS Peter & Paul Catholic Church. Interment will be in the church cemetery."

Lawrence is buried in Section H of SS Peter & Paul Cemetery in the Martin Martz lot (Lot 33), Grave A-4.

Martz Lane and McKenzie Road in LaVale are a short walking-distance from the site of the old Winchester Bridge School.

Ursula Lillian *Martz* Kuhlman 1911 - 2001

(Daughter of Martin Joseph Martz)

From her *Cumberland Time-News* Obituary of March 7, 2001, and from parish records, and from conversation with her daughter, Ursula Joan *Kuhlman* Whitman, we know the following about Ursula:

1. She was born in LaVale on November 8, 1911.
2. She died in Cumberland on March 4, 2001.
3. She was 89 years old.
4. She was the wife of <u>William Lawrence Kuhlman 1911 – 1996.</u>
5. She had four sons:
    Lawrence J. Kuhlman 1936 - 1999
    Infant Twin Boys without names (1937)
    Stillborn Boy (1941)
6. She had two daughters (Both still living as of this publication):
    Lillian Louise Gellner
    Ursula Joan Whitman
7. She was a member of the Ladies Auxiliary of Pope John XXIII Council #5450 of the Knights of Columbus.
8. She was preceded in death by 8 brothers and 3 sisters.
9. Ursula is buried at SS Peter & Paul Cemetery in Cumberland.

> Born on Nov. 8, 1911, in LaVale, she was the daughter of the late Martin Joseph and Elizabeth Mary (Marley) Martz. She was also preceded in death by her husband of over 60 years, William Lawrence Kuhlman; her son, Lawrence J. Kuhlman; her son-in-law, Fred Gellner; eight brothers; and three sisters.

This excerpt from Ursula's obituary presents eight brothers and is the only obituary that proffers eight sons of Martin Joseph, but this number, "eight," is indeed correct, for, after Ursula's birth , her eighth brother was born:

John Martz 1913 - 1913

(Son of Martin Joseph Martz)

The Eighth Son

Infant

Born November 22, 1913
Died November 23, 1913

This is information I obtained from parish cemetery records:

John is buried in Section H of SS Peter & Paul Cemetery in the Martin Martz lot (Lot 33), Grave B-1.

Lot 33 is 14 ft x 15 ft and contains twelve graves, five of which are empty at the time of this publication:

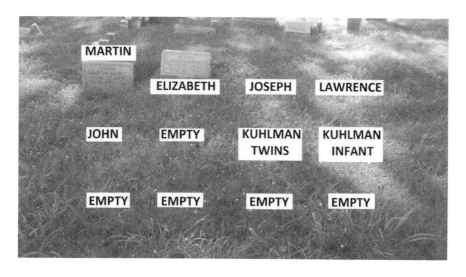

The Burial Lot of Martin and Elizabeth Martz

At the time of this publication, this plot is home to the unmarked graves of three of their children and three grandchildren.

VII

PETER MARTIN

Peter Martin Martz 1870 - 1950
(Son of Peter and Alice Martz)

Peter Martin is this writer's great-grandfather.

Buried at St. Ambrose in Cresaptown,
he is the husband of Ellen Luvertie *Cadwallader* Martz 1880 - 1974.

1981 Re-issue of 1871 Certificate

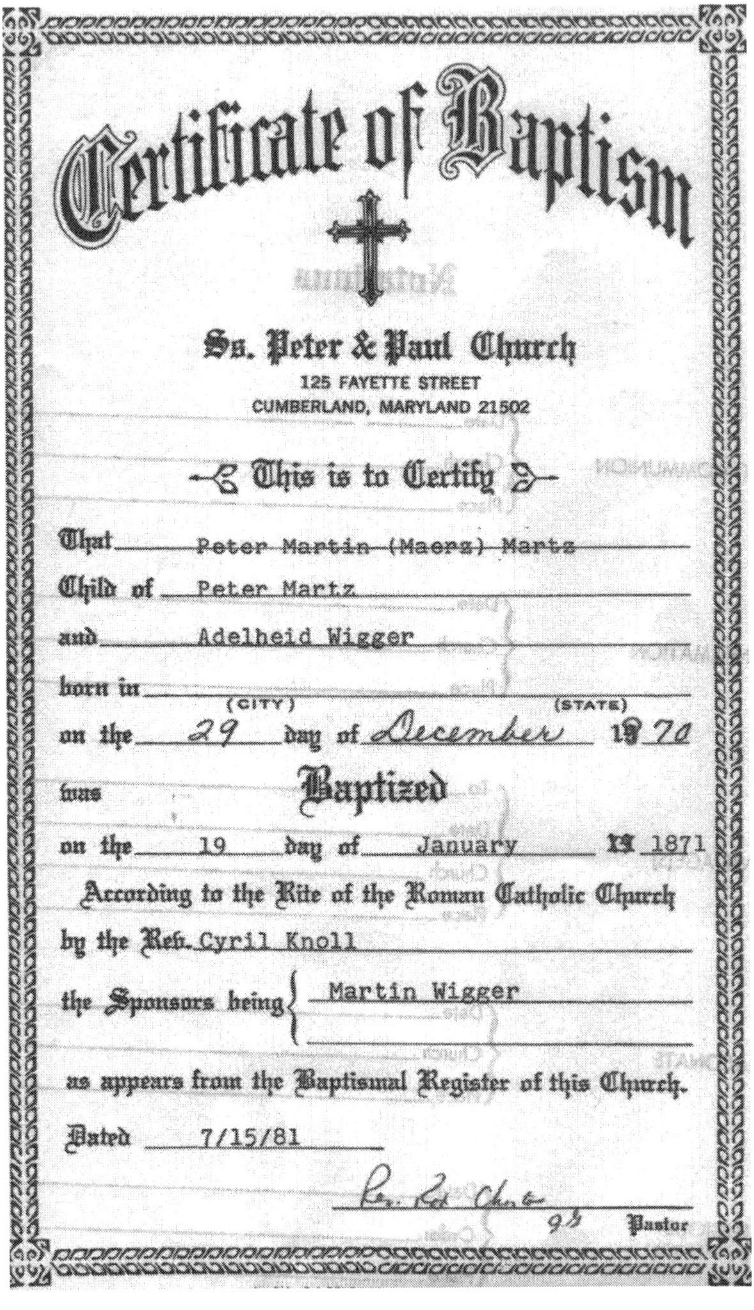

Certificate of Baptism

Ss. Peter & Paul Church
125 FAYETTE STREET
CUMBERLAND, MARYLAND 21502

This is to Certify

That Peter Martin (Maerz) Martz

Child of Peter Martz

and Adelheid Wigger

born in _____ (CITY) _____ (STATE)

on the 29 day of December 1870

was **Baptized**

on the 19 day of January 1871

According to the Rite of the Roman Catholic Church

by the Rev. Cyril Knoll

the Sponsors being Martin Wigger

as appears from the Baptismal Register of this Church.

Dated 7/15/81

Rev. _____ Pastor

Peter Martin Martz
1870 - 1950

Peter Martin Martz was 14 years old when he received his first Holy Communion at SS Peter & Paul, a church established to serve the county's German Catholics, which explains his "Communion-Andenken" or "Communion Certificate," above, being written in German.

From the *Cumberland Evening Times* obituary, Wednesday, September 27, 1950, as well as from parish records, family archives and oral tradition, I hereby proffer these basic facts that I know to be certain regarding the life of my great-grandfather, who is Peter Martin Martz, who, in our family, was always known as "Grandpap Martz":

The Children of Peter and Ellen Martz:

Pearl Alice *Martz* Hill 1898 - 1987
Julius William Martz 1900 - 1991
Franklin Edward Martz 1903 - 1981
Carolina Cecelia *Martz* Boyd 1906 - 1989
Bertie Edna *Martz* Niner 1913 - 2012
Peter Willard Martz 1916 - 2004

Peter Martin Martz and his wife Ellen operated a small farm along Winchester Road on the north side of Cresaptown, while, at the same time, Peter worked on the B&O Railroad, where he worked as a trackman for 42 years. Their little farm was home to two or three cows, a hen house of a couple dozen egg layers, several apple trees, and a garden at least large enough to help feed the children, and sometimes grandchildren, of this son of a German immigrant.

The front of their house was right along the edge of Winchester Road, so any farming was done on the back side of the property. The front of the house appeared to be a two-story structure, but the basement was fully used as a living area, so it was essentially a three-story dwelling, and, because it was veneered in stucco, any family reference to it is a reference to "the old stucco house," which, by the time of my childhood, had been taken by "eminent domain" and torn down to make way for a wider Winchester Road.

Peter was already 60 years old when the great depression hit, and, when hard times forced some of his grown children, and some of *their* children, to move back into "the old stucco house," Peter and Ellen helped to provide for them all to the best of their ability, and, by all accounts, Peter Martin Martz (Grandpap Martz) was a beloved, hard-working man who earned the respect of all of his grateful children and grandchildren.

Peter's wife was Ellen Luvertie *Cadwallader* Martz, the daughter of John and Frances *Anderson* Cadwallader. There has been some confusion regarding the spelling of "Cadwallader," for some sources have incorrectly spelled it "Cadwalder," "Caldwaller," and so on, but I am in possession of a copy of her Baptism certificate that very clearly proclaims the baptism of "Ellen Luvertie Cadwallader." Furthermore, as we seem to have no document more-authoritative than the Baptism Certificate, the most believable spelling is "Cadwallader," a verifiable Welsh name that means "Leader of The Battle."

Additionally, Ellen's rather unusual middle name, "Luvertie," is clearly verified by her birth certificate, a re-issue of which was signed in 1966 in the very legible handwriting of a competent priest, Father Carol Warner.

She was the woman I knew as "Gramma Martz." She was a resourceful woman who sold not only eggs from her chickens but also illegal beer and whiskey out of the "old stucco house" in order to further provide for her children and grandchildren, and it wasn't only bottles-to-go that she sold, for she sold also individual drinks, creating at the old stucco house a rogue *bar* as well as a clandestine liquor store.

However, notwithstanding the misdemeanor turpitude of her selling prohibited beverages, she was a devout Catholic who often prayed her Rosary and stayed in good standing with her church, St. Ambrose in Cresaptown. In fact, construction on the new St. Ambrose was able to begin in 1955 due in part to the generous contribution she made to the building fund. Later in her life, when her age and lack of transportation would inhibit her attendance at the Mass, the priest himself would bring Holy Communion to her house on Winchester Road, which by then was no longer a house of dubious repute, but now was the obviously-Christian home of the gray-haired and reformed Ellen Martz and the daughter who cared for her until her death, Pearl Alice.

By the time of my childhood she was already an old woman, though still quite lively and able to cause me to flee when she would chase me away from her apple trees, or when she would discover me teasing her rooster or making a forbidden dam in her creek.

By all accounts, Gramma Martz was rather stern and aloof, and I was almost afraid of her, yet I loved her and was fascinated with her. I especially loved the way she liked to tell ghost stories, and she was very good at it, often scaring the daylights out of us kids. She was an enigma to me, and her mysterious character inspired the following poem I would write many years after her death:

A Dark Peace

Gramma's rocker was a wooden thing,
With twisted steel-wire ties, I think.
It might have been black or nearly black,
With a spindle frame and slatted back.

Her shoes were black and business-like,
With a modest heel and laces tight.
And next to the blackened stove she'd rock:
Tick, tock, like a pendulum clock.

Her eyes were closed, but her lips moved
As she fingered beads that now were smooth
From years of honoring a solemn pact,
And the Rosary, too, was sedately black.

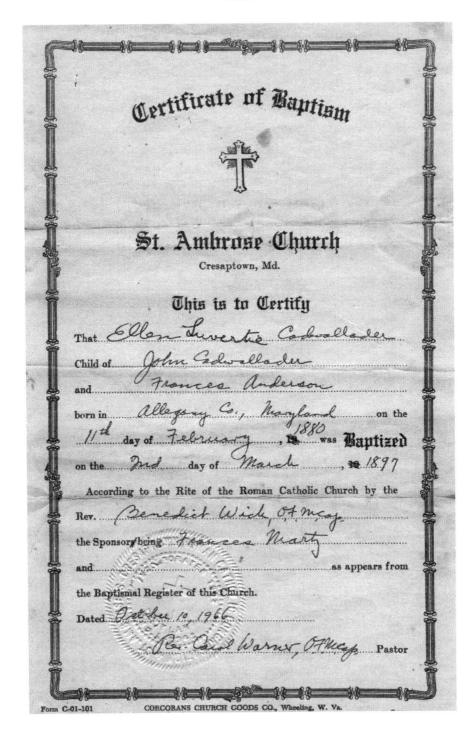

Ellen Luvertie *Cadwallader* Martz
1880 - 1974

The Wife of Peter Martin Martz
She died June 23, 1974

The Children of Peter Martin Martz:

Pearl Alice *Martz* Hill 1898 - 1987
(Daughter of Peter Martin Martz)

She was the mother of five:

Brady Dennison Hill 1919 - 2003
Ada Lee *Hill* Fadley 1923 - 2016
James Leonard Hill 1932 - 2005
Wallace Wayne McKee 1938 - 2011
Ernest Wesley McKee 1941 - Living

1. Pearl was the wife of Daniel Bradley Hill 1896 - 1953.
2. She was the firstborn child of Peter and Ellen Martz.
3. She was this writer's grandmother (Gramma Hill), my mother's mother. I spent much of my childhood with her. I loved her dearly, and I loved being in her company.
4. She was born on March 5, 1898.
5. It is likely that she was born at the "old tunnel place," a house that apparently was adjacent to a railroad tunnel along the slope on one of the foothills of Dan's Mountain between LaVale and Eckhart.
6. It seems that, by the time she was an adult, her parents, Peter Martin Martz and Ellen, had moved from the "old tunnel place" and had settled in Cresaptown at the "old stucco house."
7. On August 27, 1918, at age 20, she married Daniel Bradley Hill. Daniel was known as "Pat Hill," and he was 22 when he married the 20-year-old Pearl on his birthday in 1918.
8. My mother, whose mother was Pearl, told me that Pat Hill was a beer-and-whiskey customer at the stucco house, and that *that* is how he met the proprietor's eldest daughter.
9. After Pat and Pearl married, they lived a short while on "Red Hill," along Route 40 between LaVale and Frostburg, near the historic Toll House, but the house they rented there was destroyed by a fire from which they barely escaped by climbing out onto the porch roof and climbing down a tree adjacent to the porch. After that, they

rented the Toll House itself, not long after the toll house had retired from actually collecting tolls from travelers who would pay for the use of the "National Highway."

10. After their few years on Red Hill, Pat and Pearl moved back to Cresaptown, where they rented a house next to the old two-room school on Winchester Road, and there they began to raise children.
11. Pearl gave birth to her first child, <u>Brady Dennison Hill</u> in 1919.
12. She gave birth to <u>Ada Lee *Hill* Fadley in 1923.</u>
13. We know that Pat, Pearl, Brady, and Ada still lived beside the old two-room school when the Great Depression hit, because Ada, my mother, remembered being a little girl who used to watch the men working on the new Cresaptown School, which was built in 1930.
14. According to my mother Ada, by the time Brady was about 11 or 12 years old, and Ada was about 7 or 8, which means about 1930, Pearl had become quite disenchanted with the reckless and abusive Pat Hill, whom she then ejected from the house, after which time the two began living separate lives, and Pearl and her children, Brady and Ada, moved back into the stucco house.
15. Then Pearl fell in love with <u>James "Jimmy" McKee</u> of Cresaptown, with whom she had become familiar due to his patronage at the stucco house. Jimmy McKee worked at the local textile mill, The Celanese Corporation, and was evidently a very likeable fellow, for even Pearl's very discerning mother seemed to approve of Jimmy McKee.
16. Pearl and Pat never divorced, however, which might be understood in light of the times and considering Pearl's (and her mother's) Catholic faith, and Pat Hill was apparently very persistent, so in 1932 at the stucco house, Pearl gave birth to her third child, whom she named "<u>James Leonard Hill</u>, although, according to my mother, Pearl was already in love with James McKee.
17. Although Pearl's mother liked Jimmy McKee, there would be no extramarital affair at the stucco house, where Ellen Martz tolerated no misbehavior other than her own bootlegging, which explains, according to my mother (Pearl's daughter), why Pearl would rather often say she was going "berry picking," but would later return with no berries, for certainly the "berry picking" was an excuse for her to go off somewhere to be with Jimmy McKee.
18. By 1938 Pearl apparently had resolved to never again grace Pat Hill with her intimate affection, an affection that my mother said was then focused solely on Jimmy McKee, and on July 23, 1938 Pearl

gave birth to her fourth child, a son by Jimmy McKee, and by then, even at the risk of scandal, she had apparently resolved to assign proper surnames to her children, for she named that fourth son <u>Wallace Wayne McKee</u>.

19. Next, in 1941, she gave birth to her fifth child, and she named him <u>Ernest Wesley McKee</u>.

20. On January 28, 1953, Pearl's marriage to Pat Hill was at last terminated when he was killed at work. The Klavuhn Company coal truck in which he was a passenger was hit by a train at a crossing on Virginia Avenue, killing Pat hill and the driver of the truck. Pat Hill was this writer's grandfather, and when I attended his funeral, I was in my mother's womb and would be born three months later on April 27, 1953.

21. In family archives we have the receipt that shows that Pearl paid George Funeral Home for the funeral of Pat Hill, paying $435.00 for funeral expenses paid in full, and that she paid also for his burial plot, which is at Plot 114 at Hillcrest Memorial Park in Cumberland, where, as of the date of this publication, Pat Hill lies in an unmarked grave. I was 60 years old when I did my research and then made my pilgrimage to Plot 114, where I stood on the grassy earth that shows no sign of my grandfather who lies there, and, despite any hard feelings that might have allowed my mother and grandmother to be complacent with the lack of any memorial or marking, I found it quite unsettling that my grandfather should be so summarily dismissed, left alone in a grave unmarked and never visited. So now I occasionally visit the spot and pray, praying for Pat Hill, praying to someday have the means to buy a stone, and grateful for my own life, which, after all, I was granted through the life of Daniel "Pat" Hill, my grandfather.

22. I have no other details regarding James "Jimmy" McKee, the father of two of Pearl's sons. By the 1960's, I was a child getting about Cresaptown on foot and came to know Jimmy McKee as an old bachelor who himself got about on foot and frequented the bars, but, on the several occasions that I spoke with him, he seemed a very friendly and likeable person. He usually gave me some change each time I saw him, and I remember him as the person who gave me my first half-dollar, a single silver coin that seemed to me so huge. I had never had the privilege of knowing a grandfather, so, in my childish perception, I rather *imagined* him to be my grandfather, the man my grandmother loved.

23. Pearl Alice *Martz* Hill died at the age 89 on November 5, 1987, and she is buried at St. Ambrose Cemetery in Cresaptown. I loved her dearly, and she is one of the reasons that I am so very glad that Peter Martz and Alice *Wigger* Martz had so long ago left Germany and came to America.
24. A memory of her inspired me to write the following poem many years after my great privilege of spending my youth in her company:

Her Vegetable Garden

I think I was maybe half her height
When first I helped her water the garden:
I'd step between the rows alright,
Receiving at once her gracious pardon
For damage done by an errant step
When eagerness soared though caution slept.

I think she was proud of the pace I kept,
Bringing buckets of water up from the run,
Intent to prove myself adept
At manly work that was secretly fun,
Inwardly grunting, whistling aloud,
And ever trying to make her proud.

But overhead a billowy cloud
Attracted me to a moment's dream,
Whence never again would I be allowed
To bring up water from Gramma's stream,
To hands that worked their loving care
In a little garden no longer there.

Pearl Alice *Martz* Hill
1898 - 1987

Daniel Bradley Hill
"Pat"
1896 - 1953

Husband of
Pearl Alice *Martz* Hill

Ada Lee *Hill* Fadley 1923 - 2016
Husband Fred Nelson Fadley 1914 - 1978

Ada Lee *Hill* Fadley 1923 - 2016
(Daughter of Pearl Alice *Martz* Hill)

Ada Lee Hill was born on September 10, 1923 at the "old stucco house" along Winchester Road in Cresaptown. The only daughter of Daniel "Pat" Hill and Pearl Alice *Martz* Hill, Ada soon became the sister of four brothers and grew up in a Cresaptown where the population of chickens still outnumbered the inhabitants, most of whom carved out lives on their small farms, labored for the busy railroad, or sacrificed most of their days to the human-consuming factories of nearby Cumberland. She milked her grandmother's few cows, attended Cresaptown School, and received her sacraments at Saint Ambrose Church. The old stucco house was at once a family home and a "speak easy" under the proprietorship of a very stern matriarch, Gramma Martz (Ellen Martz), whose resourcefulness in the selling of illegal beer and whiskey helped to "keep the wolf away from the door," as they used to say so often in the Appalachian vernacular of the times, although the wolf would inevitably find his way into their lives.

In addition to the early 20th Century's systematic and normalized discrimination against her gender, Ada would survive also the many hardships of that wretched part of American history known as The Great Depression, and, along with poverty and discrimination, she would survive also the evils of alcoholism and child abuse, none of which would leave her bitter or resentful, as though no external forces had the power to invade her inner peace or to thwart her incredible ability to love even as Jesus would love: unconditionally.

Ada Lee Hill married Frederick Nelson Fadley and gave birth to six children, then became legal guardian of a seventh, and then became "Mom" to yet an eighth. Your author was blessed to become number four in that lineup on April 27, 1953:

1. Nelsie Lee *Fadley* Barrett 1947
2. Ellen Pearl *Fadley* (Thomas) Lease 1949
3. Frederick Nelson Fadley, Jr. 1951
4. Gary Edward Fadley 1953
5. Wilda Gay *Fadley* (Tice) Farley 1955
6. Wanda Mae *Fadley* (Ritz) Dolly 1957
7. Gail Lynn Williams 1966
8. Matthew Anderson 1978

In addition to these eight, Ada became virtually or nearly mother to yet other children of Cresaptown and helped also raise some of her own grandchildren. Indeed, it seemed her special mission in life was to love and care for children.

Ada passed away on January 21, 2016 and is laid to rest with her husband and near her mother in Saint Ambrose Cemetery in Cresaptown.

Julius William Martz 1900 - 1991
(Son of Peter Martin Martz)

He was my great-uncle, Gramma's brother, and he was my neighbor. I had the privilege of knowing him well, and I had huge respect for this extraordinary gentleman.

Following in his father's footsteps, Julius Martz worked the B&O Railroad as a trackman and watchman. He claimed to have started working the Railroad at age 15, which is quite believable given that he was 15 before the nation had any meaningful laws regarding child labor or mandatory education. As an adult, he lived in Cresaptown just across Winchester Road from his parents, and he was the husband of Anna May *Casserly* Martz, called "Annie," who was the sister of Mary *Casserly* Martz, who was the wife of Julius' brother Frank. In other words, the Martz brothers (Frank and Julius) married the Casserly sisters (Mary and Annie), and Julius and Annie were the parents to the following eleven children:

Five Daughters:

Shirley Ann *Martz* Baker   Mary Elizabeth *Martz* Kunkle
Betty Lee *Martz* Clarke
June Marie *Martz* Dine   Alice Geraldine *Martz* Rizer

Six Sons:

Albert Julius Martz   Leo Joseph Martz   Gene Robert Martz,
Ralph Ambrose Martz   Peter Martin Martz   Paul Richard Martz

According to parish records, Ralph was Ralph Ambrose Martz, who died October 25, 1931 at the age of 10 months and 11 days, and, for reasons unclear but possibly due to the economic conditions of the Great Depression or some other circumstance, Ralph is apparently buried at St. Ambrose in the same grave with his grandfather, Joseph T. Casserly, in a grave whose stone is marked as follows:

The "text box" below contains the text inscribed in the stone:

> Joseph T. Casserly
> 1865 -
>
> Russell Casserly
> 1909 - 1931
>
> Ralph A. Martz
> 1931
> Aged 9 mos 2 dys
>
> IN CARE OF THE SACRED HEART

As of this publication, Joseph's year of death has not been inscribed in this stone, which bears only the year of his birth, 1885. He is the father of Anna *Casserly* Martz and Russell Casserly, who died at about the age of 22, and Ralph A. Martz was Joseph's grandson, the 10-month-old son of Julius and Annie.

Peter and Paul were twins who were born and died in 1947, dying when they were 6 and 7 months old, respectively. Paul Richard Martz died November 9, and Peter Martin Martz died November 23. They were the last children born to Julius and Annie Martz, and they are buried in the same grave with their parents at St. Ambrose. Also in this same grave are the cremated ashes of the twins' adult brother Gene R. Martz, who died of cancer on April 26, 1999 at the age of 56, meaning that five members of the family are buried in this grave:

Here lies Five:

I just want to make perfectly clear that, even though only four names are presently inscribed, <u>five</u> are buried here.

Shirley *Martz* Baker, Gene's sister, assures me that they placed Gene's cremated ashes *"in the middle between Mom and Dad."*

Cumberland Times-News, April 27, 1999:

"Gene R. Martz, age 56, residing in Toledo, died April 26, 1999 at Northwest Hospice of Perrysburg, Ohio, of cancer after a short illness.

He was born July 19, 1943 in Cresaptown, Maryland.

He was employed by the Clopper Oil Company and was a manager of the Gulf service station in Bowling Green.

His wishes were to be cremated. A private service will be held at St. Ambrose Cemetery in Cresaptown at a later date."

A Miserable November For Julius and Annie Martz

Cumberland News, November 11, 1947:

Martz Child Rites

"A funeral service for Paul Richard Martz, six-months-old son of Julius and Anna May *Casserly* Martz, Winchester Road, who died yesterday morning at his home, will be conducted this afternoon at 2 o'clock in the Stein Funeral Home.

Father Cletus, of SS Peter & Paul Catholic Church, will officiate, and Burial will be in St. Ambrose Cemetery, Cresaptown.

Also surviving are several brothers and sisters."

Cumberland News, November 24, 1947:

Martz Infant

"Peter Martin Martz, 7-month-old son of Julius and Anna *Casserly* Martz, died yesterday morning at his home in Cresaptown after an illness of 10 days. His twin brother, Paul Richard, died November 10.

Surviving besides the parents are eight brothers and sisters.

The body will remain at Stein's Chapel, where a funeral service will be held tomorrow at 10 a.m., with Father Cletus, pastor of St. Ambrose Catholic Church, Cresaptown, officiating. Interment will be in St. Ambrose Cemetery."

According to parish burial records, and according to Shirley *Martz* Baker, whom I interviewed for this book, the twins Peter and Paul died from Pertussis, which is commonly called "Whooping Cough," or "100 day cough," a highly contagious, airborne disease caused by a bacterial infection that produces a violent cough that often creates a high-pitched "whoop" sound when the sufferer breathes in. This hideous disease has been around at least since the 16th Century but was not discovered until 1906. The coughing can be so violent as to cause fainting, vomiting, hemorrhages, hernias, and rib fractures. However, children less than one year old may have little or no cough and, instead, have periods where they do not breathe. Whooping Cough vaccine became available by the 1940's, the decade in which little Peter and Paul died, but vaccines are often greeted with skepticism, and they are not instantly available everywhere, so perhaps the vaccine became known, received, or available just a little too late to save these innocent babies. Paul died first, and Peter died two weeks later.

Besides the grief of the deaths of three infant children, Julius and Annie Martz had the difficult task of raising the eight children who all survived into their adulthood. Even given Julius' relatively good job with the B&O Railroad, the task must have been daunting. His efforts to feed so many children were aided by the garden he kept in the back of his house along Winchester Road. His house, like ours, was built on the slope at the foot of Haystack Mountain, but he dug into the hillside and made level terraces of earth held in place by railroad crossties, and in the growing season those terraces were the home of all manner of plump, pampered vegetables.

Further up on the hill, behind the gardens and behind the sheds, stood his arbor of equally plump and pampered grapes. When I was a child of such poverty that made sweets a rare treat, I used to love the grapes that Annie seemed to keep a good eye on. She seemed to have eyes like a hawk, and I was never able to be in her grapes for very long before she would appear at the back door, and, without even opening the screen door, she would yell at me through the screen, telling me to "get the hell out" of her grapes, and I would scurry off in sweet retreat. She never did make a big deal out of it though, and she didn't once complain about me to my parents, so, looking back on it, I wonder if she might have generously *allowed* my frequent trespassing to some extent, giving me a few minutes with those wonderful grapes before scaring me away.

As I said, Julius lived just across Winchester Road from his parents. By the time of my childhood, though, his father had died, so Julius lived just across from the house that his mother (my Gramma Martz) and his sister (my Gramma Hill) shared, a house that sat on Gramma Martz's property a stone-throw from the spot where once stood the old stucco house. As a child, there was not a day that passed without my spending some time at Gramma's house, so I would often be there when Julius would be there visiting his mother and sister. He was my "uncle" because kids don't normally distinguish between "uncle" and "great-uncle," and I was always glad to be at Gramma's when he was there. He had a presence that to me was very relaxing. His voice was not unlike the soothing purr of a contented cat, and I fancied him an unassuming *strong man* who could carry crossties and drive spikes all day as a trackman. This image was further bolstered one day when Julius showed up at Gramma's with an axe. He was on the way to the woods adjacent to Gramma's property, on his way to bring in a locust post he needed to replace a post in the fence that distinguished his property from the property of the Cecil family who were his neighbors.

After he chatted awhile with my grandmothers, Julius walked with his big axe across Gramma's fields, the fields he had grown up in, toward Dan's Mountain, and then disappeared into the woods. I was probably busy teasing Gramma's rooster and throwing rocks in the creek, so I had rather forgotten about Julius, who in time returned carrying a huge post on one shoulder and an axe on the other, evoking in me the image of Paul Bunyan. I knew that he had worked carrying crossties, and I felt so very proud of my powerful old uncle. Then, there in Gramma's dirt yard, the chickens scattered when Julius dropped that huge post to the ground. Both Grammas came out to admire the very straight and sturdy specimen of hardwood, and Julius explained to me that it was a length of *locust*, which he said was *perfect,* and I still remember how the otherwise humble Julius Martz seemed so proud of his wonderful locust post.

Mostly, however, what I remember about Julius Martz was his soothing voice and peaceful countenance. Like his mother, Julius liked to tell stories, and it was from him, my Uncle Julius, the grandson of Peter and Alice Martz, that I first heard of the attack on the 21st Bridge. As a child, I had little interest in the story. Now, however, I wish I had given it more attention, but it wasn't the story but the storyteller who had my attention.

With Annie, with his son Gene, and with his twins Peter and Paul, Julius Martz is buried at St. Ambrose in Cresaptown.

Saint Ambrose Cemetery in Cresaptown

Julius W. Martz 1900 - 1991

Julius William Martz 1900 - 1991
(Father of Eleven Children)

This painting of Julius is provided here by his daughter Shirley *Martz* Baker, who at the time of this publication still lives in the house behind which once stood the terraced gardens that Julius had built from railroad crossties at the foot of Haystack Mountain.

Franklin Edward Martz 1903 - 1981

(Son of Peter Martin Martz)

1. Frank Martz, who at the 1930 *U.S. Census* was listed as a laborer for the railroad, was born on December 2, 1903.
2. Frank was six years old when his grandfather, Peter Martz, survivor of the attack on the 21st Bridge, died in 1909.
3. Frank was the husband of Mary Lavena *Casserly* Martz, whose sister Anna *Casserly* Martz married Frank's brother Julius. In other words, the Martz brothers (Frank and Julius), married the Casserly sisters (Mary and Annie).
4. Frank and Mary had nine children:

    Edward (Eddie), who was killed at the age of 5
    Ruth *Martz* Cox,
    Earl, who died at the age of 15
    Infant Twins, who died at birth
    Allen
    Helen Martz, who died at the age of 17
    Rose *Martz* Simpson
    Mary *Martz* Markwood

5. Frank died on December 26, 1981.
6. Frank and Mary Lavena *Casserly* Martz are buried side by side at Hillcrest Cemetery in Cumberland.

Cumberland Evening Times, December 28, 1981:

FRANKLIN EDWARD MARTZ

"Franklin Edward Martz, 78, of 340 Baltimore Avenue, died Saturday night at Memorial Hospital, where he had been a patient two weeks. He had been in ill health several years.

Born in Cresaptown, he was a son of the late Peter Martin Martz and Ellen L. Cadwallader Martz.

He was a retired carpenter and block layer after 42 years of service, a former employee of the Empire Construction Company, Baltimore, and a member of Saint Ambrose Catholic Church, Cresaptown.

Surviving are his widow, Mary L. Casserly Martz; three daughters, Mrs. Ruth Cox, Ravenna, Ohio, Mrs. Mary Markwood and Mrs. Rose Simpson, both of Cumberland; a son, Allen R. Martz, city; three sisters, Mrs. Carrie Boyd, Wiley Ford, Mrs. Pearl Hill, Cresaptown, and Mrs. Bertie Niner, Pinto; two brothers, Peter W. Martz and Julius Martz, both of Cresaptown; 11 grandchildren and 6 great-grandchildren.

Friends will be received at the Silcox-Merritt Funeral Residence today and tomorrow from 2 - 4 and 7 - 9 p.m.

Services will be conducted in the funeral home Wednesday at 10 a.m. by the Rev. William Moody, assistant pastor at St. Mary's Catholic Church. Interment will be in Hillcrest Memorial Park.

Pallbearers will be Virgil Markwood Jr., David Markwood, Gary Martz, Joe Simpson Jr., Larry Stott, and Frank Hott."

Franklin "Frank" Martz And The Stucco House
(See Ellen, wife of Peter Martin Martz)

As I said when telling of the home of Peter and Ellen Martz, "The Old Stucco House," the residence served also as a "speak easy," where Ellen (this writer's "Gramma Martz") sold illegal whiskey, supplying many of the residents of Cresaptown with that which they saw as nothing less than their God-given right.

My mother told me that Gramma's suppliers were various, but that one of her routine providers was her own son Frank, who would regularly employ the cover of woods on Haystack Mountain in his clandestine distilling operation:

Cumberland Evening Times, September 17, 1930:

Three Held For Liquor Plant Ownership Here

"John Grabenstein and Eddie Grabenstein, Route No.1, and Frank Martz, Cresaptown, were arrested yesterday afternoon by U.S. Deputy Marshal James Holmes, charged with the manufacture and possession of intoxicating liquor in connection with a fifty-gallon plant seized by prohibition agents in the woods adjoining the McMullen Highway between Cumberland and Cresaptown September 12.
    Eddie Grabenstein pleaded guilty before U.S. Commissioner Thomas J. Anderson, and the other two defendants not-guilty. Hearings were set at later date and bonds posted."

Cumberland Evening Times, May 19, 1931:

"John Grabenstein, Eddie Grabenstein, and Frank Martz changed their plea to guilty, manufacture, and possession, and drew two months in jail each."

Franklin Edward "Frank" Martz
1903 - 1981

When I was a child, Frank would sometimes be at Gramma's house, the house that his sister Pearl shared with his mother Ellen, and I was often there myself. Frank walked with a limp because his leg was forever bent due to a terrible fracture he had suffered when he had fallen out of a tree while working for the railroad. Frank was a trackman, so, presumably he had been doing some tree work as part of his railroad job. While interviewing his daughters in preparation for this book, they told me that Frank had also broken an arm and other bones in that fall and that the injuries had nearly killed him. When I was a child, the story and the limp were unsettling to my childhood sensibilities.

THE MARTZ CONNECTION

He didn't come around often enough for me to get to know him well, but, when I think of Frank, I always think of the terrible deaths that befell some of his children: Eddie, Earl, Helen, and the Twins.

Edward "Eddie" Martz was only 5 years old in 1930, when Frank lived across the road from his parents' house on Winchester Road, and 5-year-old Eddie was struck and killed by a coal truck there in front of the family house, a tragedy made even more horrible by the fact that his mother actually witnessed the truck mangling her little boy.

Eddie's sister Rose told me the details, but I grew up hearing older people talk about how they picked little Eddie up from the road, and how they took him next door to Frank's mother, Ellen Martz, who, telling the story years later, would describe the horrific head injury that had killed little Eddie.

Eddie had apparently been on his way to Broadwater's Store with a note from his mother, a note telling the storekeeper what she needed. Broadwater's Store was little more than a hundred yards down Winchester road from Eddie's house, at about where Warrior Run crosses under the road. The store was actually visible from the house, which makes it more understandable that a five-year-old might be allowed to venture the trek, though most of us likely feel it unthinkable to allow such a small child to walk unattended along the macadam of a relatively busy road, and I'm certain that Mary Casserly Martz carried the regret with her to her grave.

My mother was Eddie's 2-year-old cousin when he was killed, so I'm certain that some of her earliest memories were about all the talk about Eddie, and the incident is likely to be the reason that, as a child, I never once left the house without Mom saying "Watch for cars," and I was always especially mindful of the passing coal trucks.

Frank Martz was only 22 years old when Eddie was so suddenly snatched away, and I can only imagine the terrible grief of that, though yet more of such grief awaited in Frank's future.

I often visit St. Ambrose Cemetery, where so many of my ancestors rest, and I am always given pause at the sight of Little Eddie's stone, a rather simple, appropriately small stone that bears this very terse, very poignant memorial:

Edward or "Eddie" was killed just after the 1930 Census that numbers him in the household of Franklin Edward Martz. The Census was taken in April that year, and Eddie was killed July 21.

From the 1930 *U.S. Census*:

Frank E. (Head) 26
Mary L. (Wife) 23
Edward L. (Son) 4
Ruth M. (Daughter) 2
Earl (Son) 7 Months

Cumberland Evening Times, July 22, 1930:

TOT KILLED BY TRUCK ON WINCHESTER ROAD

Five-Year-Old Son of Frank E. Martz
Has Skull Crushed on Highway

"Enroute to the village grocery store with a note from his mother clutched tightly in his hand and possibly—unless grocers have changed mightily of late—with his mind on the bit of candy he might receive, little Edward E. Martz, five-year-old son of Mr. and Mrs. Frank E. Martz, was instantly killed yesterday afternoon when he was struck by a three-ton coal truck on the Winchester Road.

The child was struck almost on the doorstep of the tiny home in which the mother and father with two other children live about five hundred yards west of Cresaptown. The driver of the truck was Henry Weese, elderly coal dealer of Alaska, W.Va.

Death was instantaneous, the child's head being crushed. Large fragments of the skull remained on the road when the officers arrived. Weese stopped the truck, with which he was bringing a load of coal from Eckhart, and carried the dead child into the tiny cottage.

Officer A.M. Spioch of the Maryland State Police, County Investigator Terrence J. Boyle, and the county coroner went at once to the scene, where, after questioning witnesses and examining the marks of the truck in the road, they released Weese and declared the accident apparently unavoidable. The marks showed that Weese had made every effort to stop the truck, and Officer Spioch said the brakes were adequate upon test. Weese said the child was watching cars coming in the opposite direction.

The child's father was engaged in fighting the forest fires raging in the vicinity and was called home. He told the officers that Weese had gone past the house at speeds of 40 to 45 miles per hour on several occasions. The officers, however, could find no evidence of speeding or reckless operation of the truck or even of negligence.

The body was removed to the Stein Chapel. Burial will be made at 10 o'clock Wednesday morning on St. Ambrose Catholic Church Cemetery."

Three decades after Eddie's death by coal truck, I was another child often sent to the grocer, having to walk down that same road with a note from my mother, and those memories, many years later, would inspire a poem I would write while reflecting on the Cresaptown I knew:

A Child on The Edge

The coal trucks roared through Cresaptown
On wheels as nearly tall as I.
They spewed their smoke and shook the ground,
A threatening thunder rolling by.

But still along the roadway edge,
Where many pets had met their death,
I'd stand beside the trembling hedge
To feel the passing dragon's breath.

The Death of Earl Martz

(Frank Loses Another Son)

Another of Frank's children who always comes to mind when I think of Frank is his son Earl, who became lost in the woods of Dan's Mountain in November of 1944 at the age of 15 and died from the freezing temperatures of a harsh November. When I was a child, the adults who spoke of the tragedy referred to Earl as being "retarded," and some would say he was "slow," but laypersons have been known to use such terms when describing anything from autism to deafness and mutism.

I don't know if Earl was ever diagnosed professionally. The cause of mutism, simply being unable to speak, can be physical, functional, or psychological, and deafness is obviously a huge impediment to the development of speech. However, a newspaper article reported he "did not attend school," and that he was "of small stature for his age," and that he was in "poor physical condition," and that he was "mute and deaf." So it seems that Earl was certainly a special child.

In mid November of 1944, the good citizens of Rawlings were like the rest of the country in that they were almost preoccupied by the headlines in the newspapers. The world was at war. Too many Americans were returning home in boxes, and America's peace and well-being were uncomfortably tied to world affairs.

The *Cumberland Evening Times* On November 13 reported that the war casualties included seven soldiers from the Cumberland Tri-State area, and that one of the wounded was PFC Robert Grove, son of Lonaconing's Robert "Lefty" Grove, former star major league baseball pitcher.

For the Martz family, however, and for many of Allegany County's concerned citizens, a more immediate, more urgent concern was reported on the same page with the war's wounded, for on that same page was announced that Frank Martz's 15-year-old son, Earl, was lost on Dan's Mountain and in grave danger:

Cumberland Evening Times, Monday, November 13, 1944:

Youth Is Reported Missing
All Night On Dan's Mountain

"An all-night search for a 15-year-old McMullen highway youth missing in the rugged terrain of Dan's Mountain was reported unsuccessful this morning by Maryland State Police.

The youth, Earl Martz, of near Rawlings, was reported missing last night at 8 p. m. when Oliver S. Campbell, a forest warden, phoned the LaVale barracks of the State Police saying that he had been informed the lad had been missing for several hours.

Troopers G. M. Rotruck and Glen D. Folk went to the Rawlings section and organized about 20 men to aid in searching the thickly wooded Dan's Mountain. The State Police and volunteers covered a wide area throughout the night, but at 8 a.m. they halted their search to rest and get something to eat.

At 1:30 p.m. today Trooper Grayson S. Dunlap reported that no word had been received of the boy's whereabouts. Both Rotruck and Folk were on the mountain along with the searching party, he said. Trooper Dunlap said that the youth was in no danger of wild animals as wildcats were about the largest ones known to be in the area, but that the extreme cold of the area was a factor to be reckoned with. He estimated the thermometer dropped into the low twenties in the Dan's Mountain section.

The Martz boy does not attend school, police said. He was wearing a pair of blue denim pants and a brown polo shirt when last seen. Trooper Dunlap said he was told the boy was of small stature for his age. The search is being continued, and the aid of more volunteers will be sought this afternoon."

Cumberland Evening Times, Tuesday, November 14, 1944:

State Police Still Seeking Missing Youth

Searchers Handicapped As Earl Martz is Reported Mute; Cannot Hear Well

"No trace has been found of Earl Mart, 15, son of Mr. and Mrs. Frank Martz of near Rawlings, who has been missing since Sunday afternoon on Dan's Mountain, according to State Police.

The Martz youth is mute and does not hear very well, according to officers, and this will handicap the searching parties because the missing boy will not be able to hear their shouts in the dense woods of the rugged mountain section in which the search is being made.

Will Resume Search

According to State Trooper G.M. Rotruck, another party of volunteers will be organized this afternoon to continue the search. About 10 acres of the forest area has been thoroughly covered by the 18 men and State Police since they started to look for the Martz youth Sunday night about 8 p.m.

The youth was last seen Sunday afternoon by Pansy Lease, a neighbor who said that he and several other children were in the woods about 200 yards from the Martz residence. The other children could not give a clear picture as to where the Martz boy went after they started back to their homes, but police surmise he must have wandered off into the woods.

Boy Exposed To Cold Weather

Dressed only in a pair of blue denim pants and a brown polo shirt, the Martz boy is exposed to temperatures below freezing, and police are wondering how he can stand the elements unless he has been able to obtain shelter under leaves or in a cave somewhere on the 2,898 foot peak of Dan's Mountain. Troopers Rotruck, Graydon B. Dunlap, and Glen D. Folk are directing the searching parties."

Cumberland Evening Times, Wednesday, November 15, 1944:

Missing Youth May Have Died From Exposure

Earl Martz, 15, of near Rawlings, In Poor Physical Condition And Lightly Clad

"The wide-spread searching of Dan's Mountain has not revealed a trace of Earl Martz, 15, of near Rawlings, who has been missing on the rugged peak since Sunday afternoon, State Police said today. They also said that the below-freezing temperatures and the youth's poor physical condition probably has cost him his life. The thermometer has been in the low twenties for the last three mornings in that area.

Hunters who may be in the woods on Dan's Mountain during the next few days are urged by First Sergeant John H. Doud to be on the lookout for any sign of the youth. The Martz boy is mute and doesn't hear very well, his parents Mr. and Mrs. Frank Martz told Trooper G. M. Rotruck yesterday, and this handicapped the men in their search as the boy could neither be heard nor could he hear the shouts of the men and youths combing the rough terrain.

A party of 75 older students from Allegany High School and Beall High School, Frostburg, along with men and boys of the Rawlings area aided Sgt Doud, Sgt. Harold C. Carl, and State Troopers Rotruck, Blair J. Buckel, and Glen D. Folk in the search yesterday. An area of two miles was probed unsuccessfully.

Sgt. Doud said that fallen leaves, timbers, and other material in the woods that may have hidden the boy were moved, and wells, cellars, and outbuildings in the Rawlings area were searched. The officer said the search will be continued."

Cumberland Evening Times, Friday, November 17, 1944:

Hunters Are Urged To Look For Youth

"The organized search for Earl Martz, 15, son of Mr. and Mrs. Frank Martz of near Rawlings, who has been missing on Dan's Mountain since Sunday afternoon, is no longer being made, but a State Police officer has been assigned to the area to continue the search, according to First-Sergeant John H. Doud of the State Police.

Sgt. Doud said that hunters are being urged to be on the lookout for the missing youth. Police say they believe the youth, who is in poor physical condition and lightly clad, is dead from exposure to the below-freezing temperatures of the last few days in the rugged mountain section."

Cumberland Evening Times, Saturday, November 18, 1944:

Boy Scouts Aiding in Search For Boy

"A large number of Boy Scouts have volunteered to search for Earl Martz, 15, son of Mr. and Mrs. Frank Martz of near Rawlings, who has been missing on Dan's Mountain since last Sunday. First Sgt. John H. Doud of the Maryland State Police said that no trace of the boy has been found. A large number of other searchers aided in the search today.

Police, who believe the youth is dead from exposure to the below-freezing weather of the past few days, yesterday urged hunters to be on the lookout for the youth who was in poor physical condition and lightly clad when last seen."

Cumberland Evening Times, Tuesday, November 21, 1944:

Rumors of Finding Body of Martz Youth False

"The many rumors prevalent yesterday of the discovery of the body of Earl Martz, 15, son of Mr. and Mrs. Frank Martz of near Rawlings, are without foundation, First Sergeant John H. Doud of the State Police said today. Some of the rumors were of a "vicious" nature, police said.

Missing since November 12 on Dan's Mountain, the Martz boy is believed to have perished due to his poor physical condition and the freezing weather of the past week. Hunters have been asked to be on the lookout for the youth.

One of the rumors was that the body had been found beneath a coal pile near his home, but none of them proved true."

Cumberland Evening Times, Wednesday, December 6, 1944:

Hunters Finds Nude Body Of Missing Youth

Earl Martz, 15, Who Disappeared
From Home Near Rawlings, November 12,
Died In Woods

"A party of deer hunters found the nude body of Earl Martz, 15, son of Mr. and Mrs. Frank Martz of near Rawlings, yesterday afternoon in Nigger Hollow at the base of Dan's Mountain about two and one half miles from the home. The boy had been missing in the rough area since the afternoon of Sunday, November 12.

There was no evidence of foul play, according to Dr. Linne H. Corson, deputy county medical examiner, who said that the boy died from exposure to sub-freezing weather sometime during the first three days he was missing. The body was well preserved but was discolored. The right arm had been eaten by what members of the hunting party called "mountain rats" and there also was evidence that the toes and the left hand had been gnawed on by some animal.

Found Near Old Road

John E. Taylor, of Rawlings, discovered the body lying about five feet from a little-used logging road while hunting deer in the rugged mountain section. Also in Taylor's party were his son, Lewis, and George W. Smith and William W. Belt, both of Baltimore. The men trudged into Rawlings and reported to State Police about an hour after the body was found.

First Sergeant John H. Doud, County Investigator Terence J. Boyle, and Dr. Corson, accompanied by a party of ten men of the Rawlings, section hiked back into the dense woods over the old logging road to the body. The trip, which required the crossing of Dan's Run several times, took more than an hour.

Taylor told Sgt. Doud that a party of six men had passed the same spot Monday but had not noticed the body. When more than seventy five men had been searching the mountain after the boy was first reported missing, the section had been scoured yet no trace found of the body.

The body of the Martz boy was lying with the feet toward the logging road and the head wedged between a tree trunk and the ground. Marks indicated that the youth had made an effort to pile up the leaves by the tree trunk and finally had placed his head under the tree. When found, the body was half submerged by leaves and a trace of snow.

The boys blue denim coveralls and polo shirt were found within a few feet of the body while his shoes were discovered about five feet away. Police were told at the time of the Martz boy's disappearance that he was in poor physical condition, and they were amazed that his body had been found so far from home in view of that fact.

Searchers were handicapped in there combing of the area as the Martz boy was mute and could not have cried out in the event anyone had come close to him, police said. Dr. Corson explained that finding the boy's body nude was not strange as he had probably become desperate and hysterical and had torn his clothing from his body.

The boy's body was placed in a rubber covering, and a pole was inserted through the straps at each end for the torturous trek toward the McMullen Highway. The men took turns carrying the body.

Missing Once Before

When the party reached the highway, Mrs. Martz was standing near the hearse sobbing in the arms of her oldest daughter. Police said that the boy had been reported missing several years ago while the family lived at Cresaptown, and was gone for four hours before being discovered.

Reports several weeks ago that the child had met with foul play were proved untrue by State Police. The body was removed to the Hafer Funeral Home, and Dr. Corson made a complete examination before issuing a verdict of death from exposure.

Born at Cresaptown, the boy celebrated his fifteenth birthday on August 25. Besides his parents, he is survived by one brother, Allen, 10, and four sisters: Ruth, 17, Helen, 13, Mary, 8, and Roseanna 5. The boy's father is a carpenter for the Baltimore & Ohio Railroad.

Also surviving are his paternal grandparents, Mr. and Mrs. Peter Martz, Cresaptown, and his maternal grandmother, Mrs. Elizabeth Barnes of that section."

According to parish records, Earl was buried at Saint Ambrose on December 7, 1944.

These stories of the tragic deaths of Frank's sons were stories I grew up hearing, and they are the stories I always think of when I think of my great-uncle Frank Martz, my grandmother's brother, who, in addition to having to bear the grief of the horrible deaths of these two sons, also had to live with the childhood death of his daughter Helen, who died of Aplastic Anemia, and the death of his infant twins.

The Author's Search For The Body of Earl Martz.

I had great difficulty finding the grave of my cousin Earl Martz, the 15-year-old son of Frank who met with such an unfortunate, untimely death in the woods of Dan's Mountain. After much searching in parish cemeteries, I began to realize that his grave, wherever it was, had probably not been marked, and cemetery records are often illegible or carelessly attended (or unattended). Preparing this book, however, I had the great pleasure of interviewing Earl's sisters, Rose *Martz* Simpson and Mary *Martz* Markwood, and the very genial Mary was confident in deferring to Rose's good memory, a memory that then solved that which for me had been the still-missing Earl.

Rose, called "Rosie," told me that Earl was buried at St. Ambrose in Cresaptown, and that his unmarked grave was one of the graves that were moved in 1954, when church property was being adjusted to accommodate the construction of the new St. Ambrose Church, and that they then put Earl's remains, along with the remains of Frank's infant twins, and daughter Helen, all in the same grave with Eddie (See Edward Martz 1925 - 1930).

Next, based on Rosie's memory, I went back to the parish records for a second and closer look, this time taking with me my thoroughly investigative wife, who then discovered a supplemental record in the form of a diagram that recorded the aforementioned movement of graves, showing that Eddie's grave had in fact been moved on February 10, 1954, and that, in conjunction with that relocation, four of Eddie's brothers and sisters were placed in the vault with him. Specifically, the diagram indicates "5 bodies all in one vault, and their sister Rose assures me the bodies are Eddie, Earl, Helen, and the twins.

Therefore, I hope that all who look on the unassuming stone marked "Eddie Martz" will understand they are looking at the grave of <u>five</u> children:

The Grave of Five

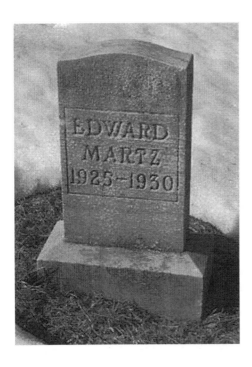

Here Lies:

Edward, Earl, Helen
And The Twins

Five Bodies
In One Grave

According to parish records, Helen died February 12, 1948 at the age of 17 from "a blood disease," adding yet more grief to the lives of Frank and Mary, who seemed destined to lose children in horrible ways.

In particular, when I consider Earl's tragic death, I think about a little boy, cold, lost in the woods, so afraid, and so alone. It troubles me such that I find at least a small measure of solace in the fact that Earl is now and perpetually in the company of his brother and sisters: Eddie, Helen, and the twins.

Jesus said: *"Let the little children come to me..."*

—Matthew 19:14

Carolina Cecelia *Martz* Boyd 1906 - 1989
(Daughter of Peter Martin Martz)

"CARRIE"

1. Carrie Martz was born on February 23, 1906.
2. Carrie was three years old when her grandfather, Peter Martz, survivor of the attack on the 21st Bridge, died in 1909.
3. Carrie had what we called a "club foot," which I think was a condition more-technically called "talipes." She had a foot, that is, that was terribly twisted and turned inward, so she walked on the side of a gnarled foot and, of course, walked with a terrible limp. Still, however, I remember her fascinating club foot stomping up and down on the piano's foot pedals while Gramma Martz sawed on the fiddle, with any adults present happily singing, perhaps in a sort of encore after a sweet history of such merriment, a history rudely interrupted by the advent of television and radio, and by the now-hectic pace of life.
4. She had two children to a man named George Myers, but this Mr. Myers seems to have been virtually lost from family history after his having given us Dorothy and Dave Myers:
5. Carrie's first child was Dorothy *Myers* Strawderman, who became the wife of the Wiley Ford Fireman that I knew only as "Brownie Strawderman," and I think "Brownie" was his actual name and not a nickname. My favorite memory of Brownie and Dorothy is of the time some of us Fadley kids rode all the way to Watermelon Park in Virginia to see a Blue Grass show starring Don Reno and Red Smiley. I might have been five or six years old when I met these icons of Bluegrass whom I had known through their television show, but meeting them was not the highlight of the day for me. Instead, the thing that I was most excited about was my riding in the back of that pickup the 150 mile roundtrip in those days in which we never allowed the notion of "safety" to put a damper on the fun.
6. The other child of the temporary union of Carrie Martz and George Myers, was the very memorable David Myers, called "Dave," who was born on March 25, 1931, who was often at

Gramma's house, and whom I considered more of an uncle than a cousin.

7. After George, Carrie married <u>Bernard Russell Boyd 1895 - 1961</u>, and the name Boyd was the name she would carry to the grave.
8. Carrie and Bernard "Russell" Boyd had a son named <u>Roger Dale Boyd</u>, who was born on October 14, 1943, who entered the U.S. Army in 1965, and who survived his military service but was killed in an automobile accident on winding Route 956 between Pinto and Short Gap on Christmas Eve in 1974 at the age of 31.
9. Carrie *Martz* Boyd died on June 21, 1989 at the age of 83 and is buried in Abe Cemetery on Dividing Ridge Road, which is off of Old Furnace Road between Wiley Ford and Short Gap, West Virginia, and her son David is also buried there.

The Children of Carolina "Carrie" Cecelia *Martz* Boyd:

Dorothy *Myers* Strawderman
October 2, 1926 - December 2, 1992
Abe Cemetery
Old Furnace Road
Short Gap, WV

William David Myers
March 25, 1931 - May 29, 1983
Abe Cemetery
Old Furnace Road
Short Gap, WV

Roger Dale Boyd
October 14, 1943 - December 24, 1974
Shenandoah Memorial Park
Winchester, VA

The Name of Carrie

When Carrie died in 1989 at the age 83, I was 36, and I had known her since my childhood, and I never heard her called by any name except "Carrie." While researching for this book, however, I came across substantial evidence that the name of "Carrie" is in fact a nickname. For example, even though Carrie's own obituary refers to her as "Carrie Cecelia Boyd," she is mentioned in her daughter's obituary as "Carolina Martz":

Cumberland Times News, June 22, 1989:

"Mrs. **Carrie Cecelia Boyd**, 83, Frostburg Village Nursing Home, formerly of Cresaptown, died Wednesday, June 21, 1989 at Frostburg Community Hospital.

Born Feb. 23, 1906 in Cresaptown, she was a daughter of the late Peter M. and Bertie (Cadwalder) Martz.

She was preceded in death by two husbands, George M. Myers and Bernard R. Boyd, and by two sons.

Mrs. Boyd was a member of St. Ambrose Catholic Church.

Surviving are one daughter, Mrs. Dorothy Strawderman, Wiley Ford; two step daughters, Mrs. Gladys Longerbeam and Mrs. Edna Printz, both of Berryville, Va.; two brothers, Julius Martz, Cumberland, and Peter Martz, Winchester Road; one sister, Mrs. Bertie Niner, Pinto; six grandchildren and six great-grandchildren...."

Carrie's Daughter, Dorothy Mae *Myers* Strawderman

Cumberland Times News, December 3, 1992:

"Dorothy Mae Strawderman, 66, of Wiley Ford, died Wednesday, December 2, 1992 in Memorial Hospital, Cumberland.

Born October 2, 1926 in Cumberland, she was the daughter of the late **Carolina Martz**. She was preceded in death by two brothers, Roger Dale Boyd and David Myers.

Mrs. Strawderman was a homemaker.

Survivors include her husband, Brownie L. Strawderman; a son, Larry L. Strawderman, Wiley Ford; two daughters, Wilma L. Wilson, Wiley Ford, and Donna R. McKinley, Cresaptown…."

———

The U.S. Social Security Death Index:

Carolina M. Boyd 23 Feb 1906 - 21 Jun 1989
SSN 215-68-6610

———

The U.S. Social Security Applications and Claims Index:

Carrie Cecelia Boyd 23 Feb 1906 - 21 Jun 1989
SSN 215-68-6610

———

It's obvious, then, that we can't always rely on obituaries and public records to clarify any doubt regarding names. I think, however, that the evidence tells us that "Carrie" is a nickname for "Caroline" or "Carolina," though I know she was almost exclusively known as "Carrie."

Carrie's Son, David William Myers
(Called "Braze," pronounced "Brazz")

Cumberland Evening Times, May 31, 1983:

"David William (Braze) Myers, 52, of Wiley Ford, WV, died Sunday at Memorial Hospital.

Born March 25, 1931 in Cresaptown, he was a son of the late George Myers and Carrie *Martz* (Myers) Boyd, with whom he resided.

Mr. Myers was a former employee of Price Beer Distributors, Frostburg; Norman Haymaker, a horse trainer in Charles Town, WV, and Sears when it was located in Searstown. He was a member of Cresaptown Aerie 2883, Fraternal Order of Eagles, and Loyal Order of Moose 948, Charles Town.

His wife, Mrs. Doris L. Coughenour, predeceased him. He served in the U.S. Army from 1949 until 1952.

Surviving besides his mother are one sister, Mrs. Dorothy Strawderman, also of Wiley Ford; a stepbrother, William Boyd, Winchester, VA; two step sisters, Mrs. Gladys Boyd, Berryville, VA, and Mrs. Edna Pentz also of Winchester.

The body is at the Scarpelli Funeral Home, where friends will be received from 7 to 9 p.m. on Tuesday. A funeral service will be conducted there at 1 p.m. Wednesday by the Rev. Harold McClay Jr. of the Cresaptown United Methodist Church. Burial will follow in the Abe Cemetery near Ridgeley.

Pallbearers will be James Hill Sr., Jamey Hill, Ernie McKee, Wesley McKee, Wallace McKee, and Fred Fadley.

Honorary pallbearers will be Gary Fadley and Bill Wilson."

Carrie's Son, Roger Dale Boyd
(Killed on Christmas Eve)

Cumberland News, December 27, 1973

"A Wiley Ford man was fatally hurt and his wife injured in a car-truck collision about 5:30 p.m. Christmas Eve about two miles south of the Old Furnace Road on West Virginia Route 28.

Roger Dale Boyd Sr., 31, the operator of the car, was pronounced dead on arrival at Memorial Hospital. His wife, Jo Ann Boyd, 25, was reported in "fair" condition last night in Memorial Hospital.

The other driver, Edwin Thomas Canan, 54, of Fort Ashby, apparently was not injured.

The victim's car and Mr. Canan's pickup were demolished in the mishap, police said.

According to Trooper Joe Siler of the West Virginia State Police, the victim was traveling north on Route 28, and, as he rounded a curve at the old Rod and Gun Club, his 1970-model car slid sideways, colliding with the pickup operated by Mr. Canan.

No charges have been preferred, Trooper Siler said, but the accident remains under investigation.

Mr. Boyd and his wife were brought to the local hospital by ambulances from Fort Ashby and Ridgeley.

Mr. Boyd was born October 14, 1943 at Cresaptown. A son of Carrie Cecelia *Martz* Boyd and the late Bernard R. Boyd. He was employed by Smith Transfer Company.

Also surviving are his widow, Jo Ann *Carroll* Boyd; two sons, Darrin Boyd and Roger D. Boyd Jr., both at home; one daughter, Tina Marie Boyd, at home; two half-brothers, David W. Myers, Laurel; William Boyd, White Post, Virginia, and one sister, Mrs. Dorothy Mae Strawderman, Wiley Ford; and two half sisters, Mrs. Gladys Longerbeam, Berryville, Va., and Mrs. Edna Tentz, Winchester.

Services will be conducted today at 10 a.m. at the Scarpelli Funeral Home by Rev. Dr. Emora Brannan. Interment will be in Shenandoah Memorial Park, Winchester."

Bertie Edna *Martz* Niner 1913 - 2012
(Daughter of Peter Martin Martz)

1. Bertie was 99 years old.
2. Bertie was named for her mother, Ellen Luvertie *Cadwallader* Martz, who was called "Bertie."
3. Bertie Edna *Martz* Niner was born on September 22, 1913.
4. Her husband was <u>George Thomas Niner 1906 - 1987.</u>
5. Bertie and George had four children:
    Eleanor *Niner* Winebrenner
    Patricia *Niner* Scott
    Richard "Dick" Niner
    James "Jim" Niner
6. Bertie was an active member of St. Ambrose Church in Cresaptown.
7. She was a member of the St. Ambrose Ladies Club.
8. She always helped with the St. Ambrose Harvest fest, and was a great cook who was known for her pies and rolls.
9. She died on May 2, 2012.
10. Her Requiem Mass was celebrated at St. Ambrose.
11. She is buried in the St. Ambrose Cemetery.

Bertie Edna *Martz* Niner 1913 - 2012

George and Bertie *Martz* Niner lived on Niners Lane in Pinto.

Peter Willard Martz 1916 - 2004

(Son of Peter Martin Martz)

Peter Willard Martz was born on May 4, 1916.

1. He was called "Pete."
2. As a child, he once lived in the historic Toll House on Red Hill in LaVale, where he lived with his adult sister, Pearl Alice *Martz* Hill.
3. He became the husband of Josephine Nealis *Hott* Martz 1918 - 2000.
4. Pete and Josephine had two sons:
    Willard Allen Martz 1939 - 2005
    Peter Martin Martz (Living as of this publication)
5. Peter Willard "Pete" Martz was a U.S. Navy veteran of WWII era, stationed at Banana River in Florida.
6. He once worked at Celanese Corporation in Cresaptown, after which he worked for Air-flow Roofing and Siding.
7. He died at the age of 87 on March 27, 2004.
8. He was a member of St. Ambrose Church in Cresaptown.
9. Pete and Josephine are buried in St. Ambrose Cemetery.

Peter Willard Martz, the husband of Josephine, is Peter III in terms of his succession from Peter Martz the survivor of the attack on the 21st Bridge.

When Peter Willard Martz and Josephine had their second-born son, they named him Peter, after his father and grandfathers before him. This Peter Martz, Peter IV in this history, distinguished himself while serving his country in Vietnam, and that service is capsulated in the newspaper article two pages forward.

Brothers Willard and Pete Martz

Willard and Pete, Sons of Peter Willard Martz, at Their House Just Across Winchester Road From The Old Stucco House, About a Dozen Years Before Pete Would Distinguish Himself in Vietnam

Cumberland Evening Times, June 19, 1969:

Local Man Winner of Bronze Star

"SP/4 Peter M. Martz, 21, son of Mr. and Mrs. Peter W. Martz, Cresaptown, was returned home after serving a year in Vietnam. With the armed forces. He received an honorable discharge at Ft. Lewis, Washington on Monday.

He has been presented the Bronze Star Medal and the Army Commendation Medal for meritorious service in Vietnam.

A 1966 graduate of Allegany High School, he entered the Army in November of 1967 and took basic training at Ft. Bragg, NC. He took advanced training at Ft. Monroe, Virginia.

In June of 1968 he was assigned to Vietnam and served three months as an infantryman. Later, he was assigned administrative duties at Chu Lai, 40 miles south of Da Nang, which is the headquarters of the Americal Division."

Distinctive Shoulder Insignia of The "Americal Division"

The 23rd Infantry Division, active from 1942 to 1971, had the distinctive nickname of the "Americal Division," and "Americal" is a contraction of "American, New Caledonian Division," a result of its origin on the Island of New Caledonia in WWII.

Peter Martin Martz 1870 - 1950
Peter Willard Martz 1916 - 2004
Ellen *Cadwallader* Martz 1880 - 1974

VIII

CATHERINE ELIZABETH

"KATE"

Catherine Elizabeth *Martz* Duffner
1874 - 1951
(Daughter of Peter and Alice Martz)

Catherine was a member of the 3rd Order of St. Francis.

To her friends and family, she was "Kate."

Born in Cresaptown at the "old Matz place," March 26, 1874.
Died at the age of 77 in Syracuse, New York on June 14, 1951.

Buried at the *Assumption Cemetery and Mausoleum* in Syracuse, New York, she is the only child of Peter and Alice to not be buried in Allegany County.

1981 Re-issue of 1874 Certificate

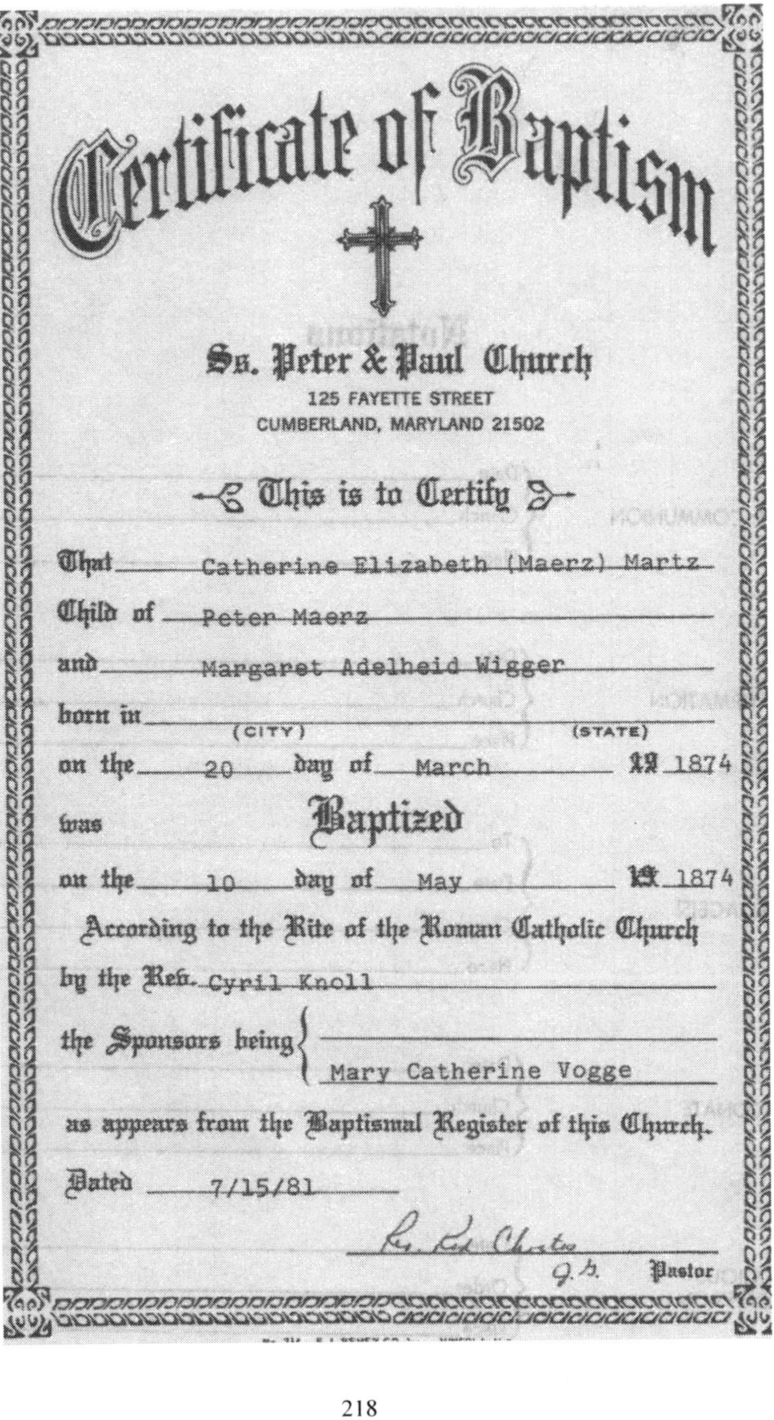

Certificate of Baptism

Ss. Peter & Paul Church
125 FAYETTE STREET
CUMBERLAND, MARYLAND 21502

— This is to Certify —

That Catherine Elizabeth (Maerz) Martz

Child of Peter Maerz

and Margaret Adelheid Wigger

born in _____ (CITY) _____ (STATE)

on the 20 day of March 1874

was **Baptized**

on the 10 day of May 1874

According to the Rite of the Roman Catholic Church

by the Rev. Cyril Knoll

the Sponsors being { Mary Catherine Vogge

as appears from the Baptismal Register of this Church.

Dated 7/15/81

_____ Pastor

Catherine Elizabeth *Martz* Duffner
1874 - 1951
"Kate"

She sent many postcards from New York to Cresaptown, to her sister-in-law Ellen Martz.

I don't know how Catherine Elizabeth Martz ended up in New York, where she worked as a domestic servant in the home of the John Maxwell family in Syracuse, apparently before marrying the love of her life. That love was <u>Erhardt Valentine Duffner</u>, a German immigrant from Baden, Germany who met Catherine shortly after his arrival in this country, and their marriage was blessed with a single child, a daughter they named Marie Magdelene (Marie Magdelene *Duffner* Cady).

1900

From the 1900 *U.S. Census* we learn the following facts about the residents in the home of <u>John Maxwell</u> in Ward 12, Syracuse, New York:

John Maxwell (Head of House), 49, Mechanical Engineer
Ella Maxwell (Wife) 48,
William Maxwell (Son), 23, College Student
Kenneth Maxwell (Son), 11, Student
Phoebe Chase (Mother-in-Law), 82
Catherine Martz (Servant), 26

From that, we can see that our Kate was already in New York by 1900, but, even though she would apparently continue her employment in domestic service, she would soon be married and no longer living in the Maxwell home, for in 1904 Kate *Martz* Duffner became the mother of Marie Magdalene Duffner.

1920

From the 1920 *U.S. Census,* we learn the following facts about the residents of the home of <u>Erhardt Valentine Duffner</u> where he was renting at 1203 Park Street in Syracuse, New York:

Erhardt (Head of House), 48, Moulder in a Foundry
Catherine (Wife), 45
Marie (Daughter), 15

1930

From the 1930 *U.S. Census* we learn the following facts about the residents of the home of <u>Erhardt Valentine Duffner</u> at 1203 Park Street in Syracuse, New York:

Erhardt Duffner (Head of House), 59, Laborer in Auto Industry
Catherine Duffner (Wife), 56, Cleaner in Private Homes

1940

From the 1940 *U.S. Census* we learn the following facts about the residents of the home of <u>Erhardt Valentine Duffner</u> at 4817 South Salina Street in Syracuse, New York:

Erhardt Valentine Duffner (Head of House), 69
Catherine Duffner (Wife), 66

In this 1940 census there is no indication of employment for Erhardt and Kate, who were presumably retired at this point:

Following their marriage, according to Anne Cady, who is Kate's great-granddaughter, Catherine and Erhardt lived for a time on the Wagner farm and on Park Street in the Liverpool area. Their daughter Marie was born at the Wagner farm home.

Catherine, or "Kate" as she was called, returned to her Maryland roots frequently. She would often bring her daughter Marie and spend a couple of months in Cumberland, often with the Boch family. Many of the Maryland relatives would also come north to the cottage her daughter's family owned on Lake Ontario in New York.

Catherine and Erhardt belonged to the Catholic Church, and Catherine was very dedicated to her religion. She would sit in her rocking chair with her beads, saying the Rosary.

She was a member of the Loyal Christian Benefit Association, the Altar & Rosary Societies of Saint James Church, and was a member of the 3rd Order of St. Francis.

A member of the 3rd Order is one who shares in the spirit of the Franciscans while in secular life, and strives for religious perfection under the higher direction of the Franciscans.

The San Damiano Cross of The Franciscans

Kate was a member of the tertiary order.

Catherine Elizabeth *Martz* Duffner
Erhardt Valentine Duffner

Cumberland Evening Times, June 15, 1951:

Mrs. Catherine Duffner

"Mrs. Catherine Duffner, about 76, a native of Cumberland and widow of Erhardt Duffner, died suddenly following a heart attack at her home in Syracuse, N.Y..

She was the daughter of the late Peter and [Alice] Martz of Cumberland. She left Cumberland when a young girl but visited here many times. She leaves a daughter, Mrs. Marie Cady, and a grandson, Joseph Cady, both of Syracuse; a sister, Mrs. Fannie McBee, Westernport, and a number of nieces and nephews here.

The funeral will be held in Syracuse Monday morning."

The Cumberland paper had a Cresaptown section in which Kate was mentioned again four days after her death:

Cumberland Evening Times, June 18, 1951:
Cresaptown

"Mr. and Mrs. Edgar Winter are attending the funeral of his aunt, Mrs. Catherine Duffner, in Syracuse, N.Y."

Edgar is William Edgar "Ed" Winter 1906 - 1980, the grandson of Mary Catherine *Martz* Grabenstein. Ed and his wife Ethel used to spend their summers in New York at Marie Duffner Cady's cottage on Lake Ontario.

The Child of Catherine Elizabeth *Martz* Duffner:

Marie Magdelene *Duffner* Cady 1904 - 1991
(Daughter of Catherine Elizabeth *Martz* Duffner)

Marie Magdelene Duffner
The Daughter of
Catherine Elizabeth Martz Duffner

From family stories, newspaper obituaries, and the memory and personal knowledge of Anne Cady, Marie Magdelene's granddaughter, we know the following:

As a child, Marie Magdelene *Duffner* Cady often came to Cumberland with her mother Kate, where they would stay sometimes for months at a time, usually with the Boch family. Her mother's sister, of course, was Anna Catherine *Martz* Boch.

Marie grew up and married Joseph George Cady in New York, and they had a son named Joseph George Cady, Jr., but Joseph George Cady, Sr. died young in 1935, leaving Marie a young widow with a small son. Following the death of her husband, Marie completed her education to become a teacher in the Syracuse school system. She then received her bachelor's degree from Syracuse University (Magna Cum Laude) in secondary education in 1944 and her Master's Degree from Syracuse University in 1953, and she was a teacher in the Syracuse school system from 1939 to 1958.

In 1969 she developed a high school course for the Syracuse schools to incorporate Black History into the school curriculum, using two famous Black historians as resource people: Dr. John Hope Franklin and Dr. Benjamin Quarles.

In later years she was very active in the issues involving senior citizens and was voted Senior Citizen of The Year for Onondaga County by the Metropolitan Commission on Aging in 1978, and she served as vice president of the commission as well.

She enjoyed traveling and generally took a trip every year with whatever tour group sounded interesting to her, and she enjoyed playing Mrs. Clause at Christmas at the elementary school near her home.

The family cottage on Lake Ontario was always an important part of her life, and she enjoyed having people up to visit and to play bridge. She spent each summer at the cottage until the 1980's.

In 1981 she suffered injuries when a handyman attacked her there while attempting to steal her purse, and she was never quite the same outgoing person after that, and she died in Maryland on May 16, 1991.

Marie Magdelene *Duffner* Cady, as stated above, had a son who was Joseph George Cady Jr., who had a daughter named Anne Cady, who, in addition to being this writer's cousin, has become a *Find a Grave* friend of mine, and she sent me a message of which the following is a part:

"... I've been in contact with many of the descendants over the years. In addition to my grandmother who was the daughter of Catherine *Martz* Duffner, I was also very close to Edgar Winter, grandson of Mary Catherine *Martz* Grabenstein, another daughter of Peter. Ed [Edgar] was like a grandfather to me, and he and his wife Ethel spent every summer with my grandmother in upstate NY (I spent my summers with them)"

--Anne Cady
Granddaughter of Marie Magdalene *Duffner* Cady

Marie Magdelene *Duffner* Cady

Syracuse Herald Journal, May 21, 1991:
Syracuse, New York

Marie M. Cady

"Marie M. Cady, a retired teacher with the Syracuse School system, died May 16 at Sharon Nursing Home, Olney, Md. She was 87 and lived on Blackberry Road, Liverpool before moving to Olney in 1986.

Mrs. Cady retired from teaching in 1970 as supervisor of Social Studies for the city schools. In 1978 she was named Senior Citizen of The Year by the Metropolitan Commission on Aging.

Mrs. Cady was born in Syracuse and was a graduate of Syracuse University. Her husband, Joseph G. Sr., died in 1935.

Surviving are her son, Joseph G. of Bethesda, Md; and two granddaughters, Kelley Simonsen of Fort Collins, Colo., and Anne Cady of Manassas, Va.

Services were Monday at United Church of Christ, Bayberry. Burial was in Weedsport Rural Cemetery, Weedsport."

THE MARTZ CONNECTION

IX

MARGARET ADELINDE

"MAGGIE"
"MAG"

Margaret Adelinde *Martz* Metzner
1877 - 1949
(Daughter of Peter and Alice Martz)

Margaret, who was called either "Mag" or "Maggie," was born at the "old Matz place" in Cresaptown on August 19, 1877.

In 1897, she became the wife of John Metzner 1868 - 1925, and they lived in the Winchester Bridge area between Cresaptown and LaVale. Maggie had seven children:

[Peter Robinson]
Joseph
Marie
Leo
Agnes
Andrew
Margaret

THE MARTZ CONNECTION

1981 Re-issue of 1877 Certificate

Certificate of Baptism

Ss. Peter & Paul Church
125 FAYETTE STREET
CUMBERLAND, MARYLAND 21502

— This is to Certify —

That Margaret Adelheid (Marz) Martz
Child of Peter Martz
and Adelheid Wigger
born in _____ (CITY) _____ (STATE)
on the 19 day of August 1877
was **Baptized**
on the 30 day of September 1877
According to the Rite of the Roman Catholic Church
by the Rev. Francis
the Sponsors being { Margaret Rohmann
as appears from the Baptismal Register of this Church.
Dated 7/15/81

Rev. Rod Chester
Pastor

Margaret "Maggie" *Martz* Metzner
John Metzner

Maggie Metzner

From parish records, I found that Margaret died in 1949 from that which the priest, Father Cletus, referred to as "Dropsy," which was a term used for the condition known today is as "Edema."

Cumberland Evening Times, August 2, 1949:

"Mrs. Margaret Metzner, 71, died following a lingering illness at her home today on Vocke Road.

She was a daughter of the late Peter and Margaret Martz. Her husband, the late John Metzner, died 24 years ago. Mrs. Metzner was a member of Saint Ambrose Church in Cresaptown.

Survivors include two sons, Andrew L. Metzner, at home, and Joseph Metzner, this city; three daughters, Mrs. Marie Holt, Mt. Savage, Mrs. Margaret Bucklew, and Mrs. Agnes Wright, at home; a brother, Peter Martz, Cresaptown; two sisters, Mrs. Frances McBee, Westernport, and Mrs. Catherine Duffner, Syracuse, NY; 11 grandchildren and four great-grandchildren.

The body is at the residence.

A Requiem Mass will be celebrated at 9 a.m. Thursday at St. Ambrose Church, and burial will be in the parish cemetery."

As previously stated, I find it interesting that Margaret Martz married John Metzner, as her brother Heinrich married Annie Metzner, a point settled by John Metzner's obituary, which mentions his sister "Mrs. Anna Martz," indicating this Martz brother and sister (Heinrich and Margaret) married a Metzner brother and sister (John and Annie):

Cumberland Evening News, April 13, 1925:

John Metzner

"John Metzner, 57 years of age, died at his home near Winchester Bridge early Sunday morning. He is survived by his widow, three daughters and three sons: Misses Margaret, Marie, and Agnes, Joseph, Levi, and Andrew Metzner.

He also leaves a sister, Mrs. Anna Martz.

The funeral will take place 9 o'clock Wednesday morning from St. Ambrose Church, Cresaptown."

The Children of Margaret Adelinde *Martz* Metzner:

Peter "Martz" Robinson 1895 - 1899
(Son of Margaret Adelinde *Martz* Metzner)

In the list of her children, several pages back, the name of Peter Robinson is in brackets because Margaret *Martz* Metzner, who did not marry until 1897, apparently gave birth to a child in 1895 at the age of seventeen, *before* she was married, a child who would live only four years.

This child, otherwise obscure, was revealed to me in March of 2017 when Teresa Savage, granddaughter of Frances *Martz* McBee and daughter of Elizabeth *McBee* Lupis, provided me with the baptism certificate of her aunt, Margaret *Martz* Metzner. On the back of that certificate, in handwriting that Teresa knows to be her mother's, it is written:

"Her baby Peter Martz born out
of wedlock March 14, 1895.
Godparents Peter Martz + wife
died 1899.   Aunt Mag was 17 years old."

Elizabeth's words, above, written on the back of Margaret's baptism certificate, correctly states that Margaret was 17 upon the birth of this baby in 1895, a boy whom the family evidently called "Peter Martz," a boy whom we now know to have been Peter Robinson.

A child born out of wedlock was quite a scandal in those days, so the fact of his existence, and the truth regarding his biological parentage might well have been kept secret, making it even more difficult to find any official record of this child, but it seems that Elizabeth was determined to leave at least *this* record of her aunt's precious child. If that is the case, then I am pleased by way of *my* words to perpetuate Elizabeth's noble intentions in that regard, for even worse than an error or the recording of a so-called "scandal" is the terrible notion of denying *anyone* his rightful place in family history.

This child, as previously indicated in the list of Margaret's children, is presumably her first-born child, a baby whose birth was described in the 19th Century vernacular as "out of wedlock."

It is almost certain that Margaret still lived at home up until her marriage and therefore would have been at the "old Matz place" when she gave birth to this child, and it is conceivable that Peter and Alice might have tried to alleviate the "scandal" by claiming the baby to be *theirs* and not their teenage daughter's, all of which might be the explanation for J. Marshal Porter's description of the Martz children. That is, in his book, *Hallowed Be This Land*, Mr. Porter states that Peter and Alice "raised 6 sons and 5 daughters at the old Matz place." However, we know that Alice gave birth to 10, not 11, which causes me to wonder whether the mysterious 11th child suggested by Mr. Porter could have been this secreted child of the teenage Margaret.

This is a child that probably would have escaped my awareness if not for Elizabeth's very touching sense of family responsibility, which motivated her to leave such a note on the back of a baptism certificate, and now it is my hope that this part of this book will serve to secure this child's place in family history, for, regardless of the details and circumstances that he had no control over, he was Peter Robinson, the grandson of a German immigrant whose first name he was given, a name he bore for only four precious years of life, a name that my own sense of family responsibility compels me to safeguard and secure in print, a name that might well have been lost if not for the sentimental and diligent Elizabeth Regina *McBee* Lupis and her provident daughter, Teresa *Lupis* Savage.

The 1900 *U.S. Census* reports three persons in the household of John Metzner: John, Margaret, and 1-year-old Joseph, and she at that time declared to the census taker that she had given birth to only one child. However, if a previous birth had been hidden from the public, the Metzners would not necessarily feel obliged to report such personal information to a stranger representing that which is sometimes regarded as a meddlesome government.

The Cumberland Alleganian, August 17, 1899:

"Peter Robinson, three-year-old grandson of Peter Martz Sr., died this morning at the home of his grandparents and will be buried in the Catholic cemetery here tomorrow at 11 a.m.."

NOTE:

The above obituary has Peter Robinson passing at the age of three, which we know from the preceding evidence to be incorrect, for he was certainly four, his woefully short life spanning from May 14, 1895 to August 17, 1899, as inscribed in stone still legible at the time of this publication, the stone standing near the stone that memorializes the lives of his grandparents:

Maggie's "Peter Martz" is Peter Robinson:

Joseph Edward Metzner 1898 - 1978

(Son of Margaret Adelinde *Martz* Metzner)

Twice married, Joseph had these two wives:

Vada *Dicken* Metzner
Mae *Ward* Metzner

These are his children:

Mary Katherine Metzner
John H. Metzner
Lawrence C. Metzner
Gilbert I. Metzner
Rosetta Metzner

Cumberland Evening Times, May 18, 1978:

"Joseph E. Metzner, 79, of McKenzie Road Extended, LaVale, died yesterday at Sacred Heart Hospital following a short illness.

A native of Allegany County, he was a son of the late John and Margaret *Martz* Metzner. His first wife, Vada *Dicken* Metzner, died in 1932.

He was a retired Machinist Helper with the B&O Railroad.

Surviving are his widow, Mae *Ward* Metzner; three sons, John H. Metzner, Columbus, Ohio, Lawrence C. and Gilbert I. Metzner, city; two daughters, Mary K. Kamauf, Frostburg, and Mrs. Rosetta Pendergast, Winchester Road; a brother, Andrew H. Metzner, LaVale; three sisters, Mrs. Marie Holt, Barrelville, Mrs. Agnes Swisher, Green Spring, and Mrs. Margaret Bucklew, LaVale; 22 grandchildren; 10 great-grandchildren and one great-great-grandchild."

Joseph is buried at Saint Ambrose in Cresaptown.

Marie Cecelia Metzner, Born 1901

Joseph Edward Metzner, Born 1898

Marie Cecelia *Metzner* Holt 1901 - 1984

(Daughter of Margaret Adelinde *Martz* Metzner)

Cumberland Evening Times, August 20, 1984:

"Marie C. Holt, Barrelville, died Sunday in Memorial Hospital.

Born in LaVale, she was a daughter of the late John Metzner and Margaret *Martz* Metzner.

Mrs. Holt was a member of St. Patrick's Catholic Church, Mount Savage, the Senior Citizens in both Mount Savage and Cresaptown, and Cumberland Hall of Fame.

Surviving are two daughters, Mrs. Helen Marie Barry, Middletown, and Mrs. Mary Margaret Brode, of Eckhart; two sisters, Mrs. Margaret Bucklew, LaVale, and Mrs. Agnes Swisher, Frostburg; a brother, Andrew Metzner, LaVale, and four grandchildren.

Friends will be received at Hafer Chapel of The Hills Mortuary Monday from 7 to 9 p.m. and Tuesday from 2 to 4 and 7 to 9 p.m."

Marie Cecelia *Metzner* Holt
Buried at Saint Ambrose in Cresaptown

Cumberland Evening Times, August 31, 1976:

75th Birthday Celebrated By Mrs. Marie Holt

"A party was held last week for Mrs. Marie Holt, Barrelville, in celebration of her 75th birthday. It was at the home of her sister, Mrs. Margaret Bucklew, LaVale.

Refreshments were served.

Those present were Mae Ward, Joseph Metzner, Deana Pendergast, Charles Rice, Glenda Pendergast, Robbie Brode, Anthony Pendergast, Mr. and Mrs. Nace Bucklew, Mr. and Mrs. Andrew Metzner, Mr. and Mrs. William Barry, Sr., Mr. and Mrs. Robert Brode, Mrs. Elizabeth Holt, and Mrs. Rosetta Pendergast."

Marie was a member of St. Patrick's Church, Mount Savage.

Leo Henry Metzner 1906 - 1970
(Son of Margaret Adelinde *Martz* Metzner)

April 9, 1906 - November 5, 1970

Cumberland News, November 7, 1970:

"Leo Henry Metzner, 64, of Main Street, Cresaptown, was dead on arrival yesterday at Sacred Heart Hospital following a long illness.

A native of Winchester Bridge, he was a son of the late John and Margaret *Martz* Metzner.

Mr. Metzner was a member of Haystack Mountain Sportsmen's Club and of Saint Ambrose Catholic Church.

Surviving are two brothers, Joseph E. and Andrew H. Metzner, both of LaVale; three sisters, Mrs. Marie Holt, Barrelville; Mrs. Agnes Swisher, Glen Burnie, and Mrs. Margaret Bucklew, LaVale, and several nieces and nephews.

The body is at the Hafer Chapel of the Hills in LaVale, where friends will be received tomorrow and Sunday from 2 to 4 and 7 to 9 p.m.

Requiem Mass will be conducted Monday at 11 a.m. in Saint Ambrose Catholic Church, with interment following in the parish cemetery."

Agnes *Metzner* Swisher 1909 - 1984

(Daughter of Margaret Adelinde *Martz* Metzner)

*However, see caveat on next page.

From Social Security Death Index
And Newspaper Archives:

Agnes was born September 28, 1909.
She died December 22, 1984.
Cumberland Times/News, December 24, 1984:

"Mrs. Agnes M. Swisher, 75, formerly of 807 Maryland Avenue, LaVale, died Saturday at the Frostburg Village Nursing Home following a long illness.

Born in LaVale, she was a daughter of the late John Metzner and Margaret *Martz* Metzner.

Mrs. Swisher was preceded in death by two husbands, Raymond Wright and Eston Swisher.

Surviving are one son, John Wright, Eckhart; one daughter, Mrs. Mildred Davis, Baltimore; a sister, Mrs. Margaret Bucklew; one brother, Andrew Metzner, Vocke Road; seven grandchildren and eight great-grandchildren.

Services will be conducted Monday at 1:30 p.m. at the Hafer Chapel of The Hills Mortuary by the Rev. Teddy R. Herron. Interment will be in Sunset Memorial Park.

The family will receive friends at the funeral home Monday from noon until 1:30 p.m."

CAVEAT

Uncertainty Regarding the Biological Parents of Agnes *Metzner* Swisher:

On the preceding page, I presented Agnes as the daughter of Maggie *Martz* Metzner, and I feel certain that Maggie considered Agnes to be her daughter, and that Agnes regarded Maggie as her mother, although that relationship seems to be biologically impossible.

In the 1910 *U.S. Census*, John and Maggie *Martz* Metzner enumerate their children thus:

<u>Joseph</u>, age 11
<u>Marie</u>, age 8
<u>Leo</u>, age 4
<u>Andrew</u>, age 1 month

However, <u>Agnes</u> is absent in this succession. She was born after Leo and before Andrew, but she is not listed among the children in this census. Moreover, Agnes was born September 28, 1909, and Andrew was born little more than 5 months later, on March 5, 1910. Indeed, their births are exactly 5 months and 7 days apart, making almost certain that Agnes is not the biological daughter of Maggie Metzner.

Additionally, and even more conclusively, Maggie at the 1910 census reported that, at that point in her life, she had given birth to a total of <u>4</u> children.

Therefore, without knowing who the biological mother of Agnes was, and not knowing just how she came to be in the loving care and custody of John and Maggie *Martz* Metzner, whom she considered her mother and father, we have this family mystery to ponder.

Some of us, however, know what it means to love another's child as our own, and terms of endearment such as "mother," "father," "son," and "daughter" are of the heart, and they symbolize emotional bonds that are eternal, and that run much deeper than mere biology.

Andrew Herman Metzner 1910 - 1990

(Son of Margaret Adelinde *Martz* Metzner)

Notwithstanding misinformation on various websites, Andrew's day of birth and day of death are quite clearly marked on his memorial stone at Restlawn Memorial Gardens in LaVale:

1. Andrew was born March 5, 1910.
2. He died October 18, 1990.
3. He married Stella J Elmira *Merrbach* Metzner on June 9, 1931 in Somerset, Pa.

Cumberland Times-News, October 20, 1990:

ANDREW METZNER SR.

"Andrew Herman Metzner Sr., 80, of McKenzie Road Extension, died Thursday, October 18, 1990 in Sacred Heart Hospital, Cumberland.

Born March 5, 1910 in LaVale, he was the son of the late John and Margaret *Martz* Metzner.

Mr. Metzner formerly worked for the C&P Railroad and was retired from the Kelley Springfield Tire Company. He was a member of Saint Ambrose Catholic Church, Cresaptown; the Haystack Mountain Sportsmen's Club; and the Senior Citizens of Cumberland.

His wife, Elmira Metzner, died March 8, 1988. One son, two sisters, and two brothers also preceded him in death.

Survivors include one sister, Margaret Bucklew, LaVale; one granddaughter, one great grandson, and several nieces and nephews.

Mass of the Christian Burial will be celebrated Monday at 10 a.m. at St. Ambrose Catholic Church by Father DeSales Young.

Interment will be in Rest Lawn Memorial Gardens."

From the description on his WWII Draft Card, we know that Andrew Metzner Sr. had brown hair, blue eyes, and a ruddy complexion, and that he was 5' 11" tall and weighed 175 pounds when he registered in 1940.

**Andrew Metzner
Senior and Junior**

Cumberland Evening Times, April 26, 1978:

ANDREW METZNER JR.

"Andrew H. (Andy) Metzner Jr., 46, of McKenzie Road, LaVale, died suddenly yesterday at his home.

A native of Garrett County, he was a son of Andrew H. and Elmira *Merrbach* Metzner.

Retired from the Army after 22 years of service, he served in the Korean War and was a member of Henry Hart Post 1411 VFW, California City Loom Lodge 1677, Haystack Mountain Sportsmen's Club, and Academy of Model Aeronautics.

Besides his parents, he is survived by a daughter, Miss Anna Lee Metzner, city.

Friends will be received at the Hafer Chapel of The Hills Mortuary today from 7 until 9 p.m. and tomorrow from 2 to 4 and 7 until 9 p.m."

Junior

Andrew H. Metzner, Sr., Stella J Elmira *Merrbach* Metzner, and their son Andrew H. Metzner, Jr. are all buried in Restlawn Memorial Gardens in LaVale.

The Veteran's Bronze Plaque:

The bronze plaque, such as Andrew's presented above, a common sight in many cemeteries, is provided by the *Department of Veterans Affairs* for the otherwise unmarked grave of any eligible veteran who died before November 1, 1990.

The grave of <u>any</u> eligible veteran who dies after that date is provided the plaque regardless of whether the grave is already marked.

At the time of this publication, one applies for the plaque by submitting to the *Department of Veterans Affairs*, VA Form 40-1330.

Margaret Ann *Metzner* Bucklew 1919 - 2003

(Daughter of Margaret Adelinde *Martz* Metzner)

Cumberland Times-News, August 13, 2003:

"LAVALE - Margaret Ann *Metzner* Bucklew, 83, of Roselawn Avenue, LaVale, passed away on Monday, August 11, 2003 at Sacred Heart Hospital.

Born August 19, 1919, Margaret was the daughter of the late John and Margaret *Martz* Metzner. In addition to her parents, Mrs. Bucklew is predeceased by her husband, Nace R. Bucklew; a son, Frederick R. Metzner; and stepdaughter, Eleanor Combs.

Margaret is survived by one daughter-in-law, Myrna Metzner of Frostburg; two grandchildren, Frederick R. Metzner, Jr., and wife Tammy of Ridgeley, W.Va., and Vanessa DeVore and husband Bob of Cumberland; great-grandchildren, Levi Metzner, Laci Metzner, Christie Metzner and Hayley DeVore. Mrs. Bucklew is also survived by nieces, Mary Kamauf and husband Richard of Frostburg, Helen Barry and husband Bill of Frederick, and Margie Brode and husband Robert of Frostburg, along with step-children Nace "Sonny" Bucklew and wife Marion of Bristol, Pa., and Dorothy Mango and husband Fred of Indiana; in addition to numerous grandchildren and great-grandchildren.

Friends will be received at the Hafer Funeral Service, P.A., Chapel of The Hills in LaVale on Wednesday, August 13 from 2 to 4 and 7 to 9 p.m.

Funeral Services will be held at the St. Ambrose Catholic Church on Thursday, August 14 at 10 a.m. with Father James Kurtz OFM, Cap. conducting the services.

Interment will be at Sunset Memorial Park, Cumberland.

Pallbearers will be Joseph Metzner, Rick Metzner, Terry Metzner, Mike Pendergast, Mitch Crosser and Shane Rice."

X

FRANCES CECILIA

"FANNIE"

Frances Cecilia *Martz* McBee 1880 - 1964
(Daughter of Peter and Alice Martz)

She and John Franklin McBee 1881 - 1947 had 8 children:

Frances b. 1906	Rosetta b. 1915
John b. 1907	Henry b. 1918
Clarence b. 1909	Russell b. 1919
Elizabeth b. 1912	Margaret b. 1923

1981 Re-Issue of 1880 Certificate

Certificate of Baptism

Ss. Peter & Paul Church
125 FAYETTE STREET
CUMBERLAND, MARYLAND 21502

This is to Certify

That _Frances Caecilia (Marz) Martz_

Child of _Peter Martz_

and _Margaret Adelheid Wigger_

born in _____ (CITY) _____ (STATE)

on the _23_ day of _June_ 19 _1880_

was **Baptized**

on the _25_ day of _July_ 19 _1880_

According to the Rite of the Roman Catholic Church

by the Rev. _Francis_

the Sponsors being { _Frances Martz_

as appears from the Baptismal Register of this Church.

Dated _7/15/81_

Rev. Rod Charles
J.b.   Pastor

Cumberland News, May 11, 1964:

"Born at the 'Old Matz Place' in Cresaptown on June 21, 1880, the last child born to Peter and Alice Martz, Frances died at the age of 83 on May 9, 1964 at the home of her daughter, Mrs. Margaret "Mary" Sudine, at 110 Roosevelt Street in Westernport. She had lived in Westernport 45 years. Her husband, John Franklin McBee, preceded her in death.

She was a member of St. Peter's Catholic Church in Westernport and a member of the *Sodality of The Blessed Virgin Mary.*

The Requiem Mass was celebrated at St. Peter's, followed by interment in her hometown of Cresaptown at St. Ambrose Cemetery."

1900 *U.S. Census:*

NAME of each person whose place of abode on June 1, 1900, was in this family.	RELATION.	PERSONAL DESCRIPTION.								
				Date of birth.						
				Month.	Year.					
3	4	5	6	7		8	9	10	11	12
Martz, Peter	Head	W	M	July	1829	70	M	46		
Margaret	Wife	W	F	Jan	1835	65	M	46	10	9
Frances C	Daughter	W	F	June	1880	19	S			

Pictured above is a section of the 1900 *U.S. Census* for the household of Peter Martz at the old "Matz Place," showing that Peter, age 70, and Margaret, age 65, were left with only one child remaining in the home, and that one remaining child was their youngest child, Frances Cecilia, age 19, indicating also that Francis was still single in 1900.

At the time of this publication, Kitty *McBee* Mitchell, who is Frances' granddaughter, has in her possession a family Bible in which Frances recorded certain information, among which was a note indicating that Frances married John Franklin McBee on May 4, 1904.

Shortly after her father died in 1909, Frances and John took the 74-year-old Margaret (Alice) to live with them in Rawlings, as is evident from the 1910 *U.S. Census*.

1910 *U.S. Census* for the home of John Franklin McBee in Rawlings:

John F., Head, age 29
Frances C., Wife, age 29
John E., Son, age 3
Clarence, Son, age 6 months
Maggie A. Martz, Mother-in-Law, age 75

John and Frances "Fannie" *Martz* McBee
Married May 4, 1904

Frances Cecilia *Martz* McBee 1880 - 1964

The youngest daughter of Peter and Alice Martz, Frances became the wife of John Franklin McBee, who early on was a farmer in Rawlings, but who soon had a career with the railroad, as a track foreman in his younger years, and eventually as a watchman. The 1930 and 1940 censuses have them living on Stony Run Road in Westernport.

When Frances "Fannie" *Martz* McBee was 59 years old in the summer of 1939, she was a visitor at the home of her sister Kate in Syracuse, New York, and she sent this postcard to her brother Peter and his wife Ellen in Cresaptown. She was a long way from Westernport:

STATE TOWER BUILDING, SYRACUSE, NEW YORK

I have that postcard before me as I write, and I share here the message handwritten on the back of the card:

↓

August 2, 1939

"I am up at sister
Katie Duffner's
having a nice
time going home
the 8 of August with
love to all from Sister
               Fannie

Mr. & Mrs. Peter Martz
         Cresaptown
                Md

The children of Frances Cecilia *Martz* McBee:

Frances Cecilia McBee 1905 - 1906
(Daughter of Frances Cecilia *Martz* McBee)

STONE INCORRECT:

SHOULD READ :
1905 - 1906

Elizabeth *McBee* Lupis, this baby's sister, created a list of family births and recorded this baby's birth as March 9, 1905—not 1906 as inscribed in the stone. Here in her own handwriting, taken from one of her notebooks, is Elizabeth's entry regarding the birth of baby Frances:

Additionally, although in Latin, the Saint Ambrose parish burial record states that little Frances died September 29, <u>1906</u> and was buried October 1, <u>1906</u> and **not** 1907 as written on the stone:

> Die 29 mensis Septembris A. D. 1906 obiit Francisca Cacilia fili a Joannis F. McBee et Francisca McBee, aetatis 1 an. 6 mens. ex loco Cresaptown, Md., sepulta est die 1 mens. Octobris A. D. 1906 in cemeterio S. Ambrosii
> Adnotationes Typhoid Fever
> Fr. Benedict OSB

It is almost inconceivable that a headstone could be inscribed with incorrect dates of birth and death, but the combination of parish records and Elizabeth's handwritten notes is enough for me to conclude that a mistake has been written in stone.

I have determined that this baby lived <u>1 year and 6 months</u>, because Elizabeth recorded the birth as March 9, 1905 and because the parish burial certificate recorded her death as September 29, 1906.

Furthermore, the baby's death was published is a Cumberland newspaper that declares she died in 1906:

The Evening Times, Monday, October 1, 1906:

Funeral Today

"The eighteen month old daughter of Mr. and Mrs. John McBee of Cresaptown died Saturday Night. The remains were buried this morning at ten o'clock in St. Ambrose Cemetery."

Conclusion Regarding The Year of Baby Frances' Death:

As the parish records and the newspaper are in complete agreement, we have to conclude that the stone, as of this publication, is simply incorrect.

In August of 1964, three months after her children buried Fannie McBee, her oldest son, John, went to Tri-State Memorial Company in Piedmont to purchase her memorial stone, and at that time he purchased also stones for the two of her children who preceded her in death, the babies Frances and Henry, and the contract shows that John paid the full amount for the stones on August 14, 1964.

We may never know how the mistake occurred, but we can herein secure the facts, which I hope might be helpful for someone in the future who might discover the error, although it is my greater hope that someone, perhaps even I, will have obtained and installed a correct stone even before you read these words, for Frances is, after all, one of us, and her woefully-short life remains a thing to be cherished.

The baby Frances, who was killed by Typhoid Fever according to parish records, is at rest near her mother and father at St. Ambrose in Cresaptown, a young mother and father who must have been completely heartbroken to lose their first child, not knowing they would lose yet another.

As I present the rest of the children of John and Frances *Martz* McBee, I wish the reader to know it was actually her grandchildren who either provided or verified much of this information. Interviewing for this book, my wife and I have been honored to be guests in the homes of Helen *Hannon* Amann in Westernport (Helen is the daughter of Rosetta *McBee* Hannon), Kitty *McBee* Mitchell in Westernport (Kitty is a daughter of John Edward McBee), and Teresa *Lupis* Savage in Keyser (Teresa is the daughter of Elizabeth *McBee* Lupis). These very cordial ladies were quite helpful, and I was very pleased to at last meet these dear cousins, looking forward to our continued family connection.

John Edward McBee 1907 - 1974
(Son of Frances Cecilia *Martz* McBee)

John Edward McBee is the first surviving child of Frances Cecilia *Martz* McBee, and he is buried at Philos Cemetery in Westernport.

Cumberland News, May 1, 1974:

"WESTERNPORT—John Edward McBee, 67, of 123 Greene Street, died yesterday at Memorial Hospital, Cumberland.

Born in Cresaptown, he was the son of the late John Franklin and Frances *Martz* McBee. He had been employed by the Postal Service 40 years, retiring as a carrier in the Westernport Post Office in 1965.

He was a member of St. Peter's Catholic Church, Westernport, and Piedmont Council 685 Knights of Columbus, and Tri-Towns Senior Citizens Club.

Surviving are his widow, Mrs. Josephine *Harr* McBee; four daughters, Mrs. Thomas Suter, Street, Md; Mrs. Joseph Stremel, Denver, Colorado; Mrs. Robert Mitchell, Bedford, Indiana; and Miss Jean McBee, at home; two brothers, Clarence McBee and Russell McBee, both of Westernport; three sisters, Mrs. Joseph Lupis, Piedmont; Mrs. Bernard Amann and Mrs. Joseph Sudine, both of here, and eight grandchildren.

Friends will be received at the Boal Funeral Home today from 7 to 9 p.m. and tomorrow from 2 to 4 p.m. and 7 to 9 p.m."

In the above obituary, the mention of "Mrs. Thomas Suter" refers to John's daughter <u>Mary Jo</u>, while "Mrs. Joseph Stremel" refers to his daughter <u>Margaret Ann</u>. "Mrs. Robert Mitchell" is <u>Katherine Frances</u>, called "Kitty," and, including <u>Jean</u>, these four comprise the daughters of John Edward McBee and are granddaughters of Frances *Martz* McBee.

Catherine *Boch* McKenzie, Johnnie McBee, Frances *Martz* McBee

The Daughters of John Edward McBee:
Mary Jo, Margaret Ann, Kitty, and Jean
(Christmas 1956)

John Edward McBee
Westernport Post Office
40 Years of Service

Clarence Albert McBee 1909 - 1993

(Son of Frances Cecilia *Martz* McBee)

The Herald
Piedmont, West Virginia
Tuesday, June 8, 1993:

"Funeral services were held Saturday in the Boal-Warnick Funeral Home, Westernport, for Clarence A. "Mickey" McBee, 83, of 117 Greene Street, Westernport, who died June 2, 1993 at Memorial Hospital, Cumberland.

Father Paul A. Byrnes officiated, and burial was in St. Peter's Cemetery.

Serving as pallbearers were William Metz, William Fazenbaker, Louis Newcomb, Charles Butler, Wayne Kerns, and James Naughton.

Born October 3, 1909 in Cresaptown, MD, he was the son of the late John McBee and Frances *Martz* McBee.

He was also preceded in death by his wife, Anna Mary *Daily* McBee in 1974. Mr. McBee was a WWII Army veteran. He retired from Westvaco Luke Mill with 42 years of service as an operator in the digester house.

He was a member of St. Peter's Catholic Church in Westernport and Victory Post 155 American Legion, Westernport.

He is survived by a daughter, Mary Evelyn Moomau, Westernport; three sisters, Elizabeth Lupis, Piedmont, Rosetta Amann and Margaret Sudine, both of Westernport, and three grandchildren.

Memorials may be made to St. Peter's School or the Tri-Towns Rescue Squad, Westernport."

Clarence, Fannie, Elizabeth, and John

Elizabeth and Rosetta
July 27, 1919

Elizabeth Regina *McBee* Lupis 1912 - 2005
(Daughter of Frances Cecilia *Martz* McBee)

The Herald (Piedmont, West Virginia)
Tuesday, December 6, 2005:

"Elizabeth R. Lupis, 93, formerly of Piedmont, died Saturday, December 3, 2005 at Heartland of Keyser Nursing Home.

Born February 26, 1912 in Cresaptown, Md, she was the daughter of the late John F. and Frances C. *Martz* McBee. She was also preceded in death by her husband, John L. Lupis; a daughter, Carol F. Athey and husband Gary; four brothers, John McBee, Clarence McBee, Henry McBee, and Russell McBee; and three sisters, Frances McBee, Rosetta Amann, and Margaret Sudine. She was the last of her immediate family.

Elizabeth was a graduate of St. Peter Parochial School. She married John L. Lupis on February 23, 1936 and resided on West Hampshire Street in Piedmont. She was a member of St. Peter Catholic Church. She was a dedicated reader and early compiler of family history. She participated in numerous sightseeing tours to major attractions in this country.

She is survived by a son, John V. Lupis and wife Linda, North Ogden, Utah; a daughter, Teresa Savage and husband Tim, Pearisburg, VA; six grandchildren, Jeff Lupis, Lisa Eye, Gary Athey, John Athey, Craig Savage, and Erin Amrhein; three great-grand children, Autumn Athey, Christopher Eye, and Megan Ele; numerous nieces and nephews, and a very special sister-in-law, Catherine *Lupis* Conroy, Westernport, who looked after her during her stay at the nursing home.

The family will receive friends at the Fredlock Funeral Home on Saturday, December 10 at 10 a.m., with Father James W. Hannon officiating. Burial will be in St. Peter's Cemetery.

The family requests that memorials for Elizabeth be directed to the Bereavement Committee of St. Peter's Catholic Church, 127 Church Street, Westernport, Md 21562."

Rosetta Mary *McBee* Amann 1915 - 2005
(Daughter of Frances Cecilia *Martz* McBee)

The wife of <u>Bernard John Amann 1911 - 1979</u>

Cumberland Times-News, May 9, 2005:

"WESTERNPORT — Rosetta M. Amann, age 90, formerly of 218 Poplar St., Westernport and Grandview Apartments, died on Sunday, May 8, 2005 at Sacred Heart Hospital in Cumberland.

She was born on May 5, 1915 at Cresaptown and was the daughter of John McBee and Frances *Martz* McBee. She was preceded in death by a daughter, Rose Mary Broadwater; three brothers, John, Russell, and Clarence McBee; one sister, Margaret Sudine; and a grandchild, Katherine Ann Hannon.

She was a member of St. Peter's Catholic Church in Westernport and was a 50+ year member of Court Santa Maria, Catholic Daughters of America in Westernport. She was a member of the Westernport Senior Citizens and in past years organized White Star Tours for area residences. She was also a member of the Ladies Auxiliary of Victory Post 155 American Legion. She was a retiree of Mead-Westvaco Corporation in Luke. She loved to play cards and bingo.

Mrs. Amann is survived by a daughter, Helen Hannon and husband Bob of Westernport. She is also survived by a sister, Elizabeth Lupis of Heartland Nursing Home in Keyser, W.Va.; two sisters-in-law, Josephine McBee and Helen Amann of Westernport; a son-in-law, Gary Broadwater of Woodbridge, VA.; three grandchildren, Erin Broadwater, Ashley Hannon, and Lindsay Broadwater; several nieces and nephews and a special close friend, Barbara Brown.

A Mass of Christian Burial will be celebrated at St. Peter's Catholic Church on Wednesday morning at 10 a.m. with Father Adam Parker as Celebrant. Interment will follow at the parish cemetery."

Fannie *Martz* McBee
Kate *Martz* Duffner
Rosetta *McBee* Amann

Henry Bernard McBee 1918 - 1918
(Son of Frances Cecilia *Martz* McBee)

According to parish records, Henry died October 13, 1918. He was 11 months old. Like Frances, Henry is buried near his mother and father at St. Ambrose in Cresaptown, a mother who in 1918 was revisited by the second death of a child, having lost her first baby, Frances, in 1906.

Henry Bernard McBee   Frances Cecilia McBee
Age 11 months   Age 18 months

The two babies lie side by side next to their Mother and Father.

Russell William McBee 1919 - 1989

(Son of Frances Cecilia *Martz* McBee)

Cumberland Times-News, November 6, 1989:

Former Piedmont Postmaster Dies

"BARTON – Russell W. McBee, 70, former postmaster of Piedmont, W.Va., died Saturday, November 4, 1989 at Sacred Heart Hospital, Cumberland.

Born in Cresaptown September 3, 1919, he was a son of the late John F. and Frances *Martz* McBee.

Mr. McBee was an Army veteran of WWII and was employed by the United States Postal Service for 35 years prior to his retirement. He was a member of St. Peter's Catholic Church in Westernport; a member and past commander of Victory Post 155 American Legion, Westernport, where he was currently serving as Bookkeeper; and a member of Queen's Point Memorial Post 6775, McCoole.

He was preceded in death by his first wife, Marvel *Warnick* McBee.

Surviving are his widow, Eldora *Clark* McBee; two sons, Thomas McBee, Ft. Ashby, W.Va. and Robert McBee, Swanton; two daughters, Eleanor Smith, Keyser, W.Va., and Doris Ketterman, Thurmont; one brother, Clarence McBee, Westernport; three sisters, Elizabeth Lupis, Piedmont, Rosetta Amann and Margaret Sudine, both of Westernport; 10 grandchildren, and several step-nieces and step-nephews.

Friends will be received at the Boal Warnick Funeral Home, Westernport, Monday from 7 to 9 p.m. and Tuesday from 2 to 4 and 7 to 9 p.m.

Mass of Christian Burial will be celebrated Wednesday at 10 a.m. at St. Peter's Catholic Church by Father Paul Byrnes, assisted by Rev. Harold Malone.

Interment will follow in Mountain View Cemetery, Moscow Mills. Military Honors will be accorded there by members of Victory Post, Queen's Point Memorial Post, and Kelly-Mansfield Post 52, American Legion, Piedmont.

Memorials may be directed to St. Peter's Catholic Church, Barton United Methodist Church, or Tri-Towns Rescue Squad."

Mountain View Cemetery

Mountain View Cemetery is in Moscow, Maryland in western Allegany County, in the George's Creek Valley, about 6 miles northeast of Westernport. In 2010 the population of Moscow was 240.

Rosetta McBee   **Russell McBee**
Fannie *Martz* McBee

They were all members of St. Peter's in Westernport:

Margaret Catherine *McBee* Sudine 1923 - 1994

(Daughter of Frances Cecilia *Martz* McBee)

Cumberland Times-News, June 19, 1994:

"WESTERNPORT — Margret Catherine Sudine, 70, of 110 Roosevelt Street, Westernport, died Monday, January 17, 1994 at Sacred Heart Hospital.

Born February 28, 1923 in Westernport, she was the daughter of the late John Franklin McBee and Frances *Martz* McBee.

Mrs. Sudine was a member of Saint Peter's Catholic Church, Westernport. She retired from the Westvaco Corporation out of the Finishing Room in April 1985 with 44 years of service.

Surviving are her husband, Joseph Sudine; a son, Joseph Sudine Jr. and wife Jeanne, Bloomington; one daughter, Margaret Ann Wilt and husband Lee, Westernport; two sisters, Elizabeth Lupis, Piedmont, West Virginia; Rosetta Amann, Westernport and two grandchildren, Michael and Karey Sudine, Westernport.

Friends will be received at the Boal Funeral Home, Westernport, on Wednesday from 2 to 4 p.m. and 7 to 9 p.m..

Services will be conducted at the funeral home on Thursday at 11 a.m., with Father Ivan Lebar officiating.

In lieu of flowers, memorials may be made to the Tri-Towns Rescue Squad."

It was at 110 Roosevelt Street in Westernport, in the home of Joseph and Margaret *McBee* Sudine, that Frances "Fannie" *Martz* McBee passed away in 1964, when Margaret was 40 and Fannie 83. Margaret died thirty years later, 1994, and they lie at rest together in Saint Ambrose Cemetery in Cresaptown.

Margaret *McBee* Sudine,
the daughter of Frances "Fannie" *Martz* McBee,
is surrounded by family on the gentle slope at Saint Ambrose.

The inscription on her stone is thus:

"FANNIE, YOU SHARED HER WITH ME.
I NOW RETURN HER TO YOU."

What a sweet inscription! And I feel it is a sentiment quite befitting the conclusion of this look of the descendants of Peter and Alice Martz, for indeed we might well say to Peter and Alice:

You shared them with us.
Now we return them to you.

THE MARTZ CONNECTION

ABOUT THE AUTHOR

The author is a life-long resident of Allegany County, where he lived most of his life in the Cresaptown area. His home-spun stories and poetry have appeared in *Journal of The Alleghenies, Backbone Mountain Review,* and *Allegany Magazine*. He is a Christian, an avid reader and writer of poetry, a veteran of the U.S. Army, a graduate of Allegany College of Maryland, a veteran of local theater, a firefighter with the Rawlings Volunteer Fire Department, the proud husband of retired Master Sergeant Cynthia Bray, USMC, a proud father and grandfather, and a direct descendent of Peter and Alice Martz.

The author is pictured here in April, 2017, at a pensive moment in SS Peter & Paul Cemetery in Cumberland, the photo taken by his wife during one of their many busy afternoons in cemeteries researching for this book.

Also By Gary Fadley:

UNDEFEATED

THE MEMORY BANK

A TRILOGY FOR FAMILY

ALONG THE TRACKS

JACKSAYINGS

Made in the USA
Middletown, DE
30 August 2017